AMUSEMENT PARK HACKS

"The best book for families who frequent the parks."
"Amusement Park Hacks is a great book for families to get the most thrill while visiting the parks."
Nathan Endsley - Roller Coaster Enthusiast

"Great tool to be prepared for having a great time!"
"This book contains a wealth of information for those looking to have the best amusement park experience possible."
Larry & Jean Lines -
Travelers to amusement parks,
and grandparents to five.

"Know what to know before you go!"
"Save time, effort and expense by knowing what to do before you hit the parks. You will discover insights based on years of enthusiasts' and employees' experiences. Even as an experienced park goer I found more than a few tips I hadn't taken advantage of over the years."
Tom P. - Roller Coaster Enthusiast

AMUSEMENT PARK HACKS

BEHAVIOR HACKS & TIPS FOR A GREAT AMUSEMENT PARK VISIT

Mike Kunze & Krystal Curtis

Illustrations and cover design
Mike Kunze

Copyright © 2017 Mike Kunze

The material in this book is for informational purposes only. The authors make no guarantees that every day in the park will be perfect. Also, park rules change frequently, even in mid-season. Please pay attention to signs, price changes, schedule changes, menu options, and the park's official website for the latest information.

All rights reserved. No part of this book may be reproduced, or stored in a retrieval system, or transmitted in any form or by any means, electronic, mechanical, photocopying, recording or otherwise, without express written permission from the author.

ISBN-13: 978-0-9986950-2-0

SPECIAL THANKS

The Park Hacks series began with one guy sharing his tips and strategies. It was just me, Mike, at the beginning. I quickly realized that the book would be a lot more valuable to a wider audience if other of amusement parks shared their own tips and park hacks as well. I opened up the Share-A-Hack form on the book's blogs which produced many great hacks. It also helped me connect with Krystal, my co-author for this book. Krystal was one of the first and best participants, who emerged during my search for more hacks to share.

The Focus Group

As this book's manuscript was nearing completion, we invited people who visit other parks around the country to review this work and to help ensure that these Park Hacks apply well no matter which park you visit. The request I made to them was simple, check out what we've written, then help us make this book 10% better. Man, did they come through!

I have a couple members of the focus group who are insiders to the park and asked that their names be withheld from these acknowledgments. They know who they are and I'm looking forward to geeking out about amusement parks and building a friendship with them in the future.

This is the list of those in our focus group. They are amusement park enthusiasts, travelers, parents, grandparents and generous Park Hackers who have shared their perspective and experience with us. I'm so glad they answered the call and were brave enough to read through the early manuscript of this book.

- **Dave Ehrlich** - West Chester, Ohio
- **Nathan Endsley** - Marion, Ohio
- **Jean Lines** - Columbus, Ohio
- **John Royalty** - Lexington, Kentucky
- **Kristopher Werner** - Cincinnati, Ohio
- **Timothy Berkheiser** - Elkhart, Indiana

Thank you so much, for each of your contributions! I hope you'll return to help us review the **2018 Kings Island Park Hacks** later this year.

—Mike

TABLE OF CONTENTS

Introduction   *xiv*

The Origin   *xv*
   Theme Parks v. Amusement Parks   *xvi*
   Mike's Backstory   *xvi*
   Krystal's Backstory   *xvii*
   The Code of the Park Hackers   *xviii*
   How to Read This Book   *xx*

Chapter 1 - Prepare Your Expectations   1

Getting Ready to Go   1
   Annual Parks v. Seasonal Parks   1
   Parks that Operate Year Round   2
   Maintenance Schedules   2
   Annual Passes   2

Seasonal Trends   3
   Check Park Hours   5
   Setting Expectations   5

Define Winning for Your Group   5
   Traveling   6
   Visiting Alone   7
   Alternate Plans   7
   What to Bring   8
   Preparing for Rain   10

Chapter 2 - Tickets and Pass Options   12

Tickets   12
   Multi-day   13

Season Tickets	13
Annual Passes	15
Season or Annual Pass Discounts	15
Special Food Tickets	15
Fast Pass	16
Food	19
Park Food is Expensive	19
Long Food Lines	20
Snacks	20
Packing Your Own, BYO, or Tailgating	21
Healthy Eating v. Fuel	21
Meal Plans and Special Deals	21
Refillable Drink Plans	22
External Dining Options	23
Chapter 3 - Research the Park	25
Parking	25
The Map	27
Get the Map in Your Head	27
Park Regions	28
Landmarks	28
Meeting Places	29
Transportation	29
Divide and Conquer	30
Rides	30
Shows and Live Entertainment	30
Park Policies	31
Dress Codes	31
Weather Patterns	32
Cameras and Drones	33

Chapter 4 - Family and Group Management	35
Letting Kids Explore	35
Quiz Your Kids	35
Family Locator App	36
Smartphones and Wi-Fi Communications	37
Baby Swap	37
Graduating to New Heights	38
Small Adjustments	39
ID Cards and Wristbands	39
Activity Changes	40
Special Treat or Snack Time	40
Midway Games	41
Shopping for Souvenirs	42
Handling Problems	43
Kid Melt-down Tantrums	43
Baby Problems	44
Messy Problems	45
Mechanical Problems	45
Crowd Problems	46
Walk Away	46
Check Other Areas	46
People Watching	46
Large Groups	47
Helping the Loners	47
Meal Times	47
Work Team Building	47
Chapter 5 - Rides	49
Thrill Rides	49
Ride Manufacturers	50

Physical Challenges	53
Disabilities	53
Large Riders	53
Being Trapped	54
Special Modifications	55
Avoiding Discomfort	56
Nausea	56
Blacking Out or Passing Out	57
Joint or Back Pain	57
Categories of Rides	58
Family Rides	58
Dark Rides	58
Spinning and Swinging Rides	59
Tall Rides	60
Chapter 6 - Live Entertainment	62
Acrobatic Shows	62
Stage Shows	63
Street Performers	63
Character Meet and Greet	64
Parades	65
Fireworks	65
Concerts	66
Ride Enthusiast Groups	66
Fundraiser Events	66
Chapter 7 - Seasonal Events	69
Special Events	69
Halloween	69
Christmas	70
Special Theme Weeks	71

Chapter 8 - Add Your Own Fun	72
Gamification	72
Bucket List	72
Autographs	73
Top Rides	73
Personal Challenge and Growth	73
Parkaeology	74
Recreate a Photo	75
Television Program or Movie Locations	75
Boosting a Ride	76
Track Your Steps	78
Become a Park Hacker	79
Index of Amusement Parks	80

INTRODUCTION

Amusement parks are fun places where families go to ride rides, to eat fun foods, to see live entertainment, and to spend time together. Visitors can also use this unusual, imaginative environment to relax while swimming, shopping, and people watching. Too often, families go on a holiday, at peak-season, or on weekends, not realizing those are going to be abnormally busy. Perhaps those are the only days they have available to visit the park. Maybe they believe the park is always packed and full of grouchy people and long lines. It is just the way it is.

This guide is filled with hacks and tips collected from park regulars to help you and your family get more out of your amusement park visit. The book will help you build a plan to visit on the best days and then strategically work your way around the park. By choosing wisely, you will ride more, pay less and leave happier than you previously thought possible.

Can't families just go and figure it out? Certainly some do. Since we observe families all the time who are having a rough visit, there is a need. It is for them, or anyone who wants to up their game, that we wrote this book. There are many families who are frequent visitors to the park. They already know many of these tips. I consider those people fellow Park Hackers. I invite them to share their own tips with the rest of us. None of us knows everything. That's why the website has a **Share-a-Hack form**. The variety of perspectives is always helpful. Even seasoned park experts can still find helpful tips within. Sometimes these hacks shared are ideas that wouldn't have occurred to them. I (Mike) have enjoyed trying out some of the hacks shared by others.

As you read, if something that you want to share comes to mind, please take a note and share it with us using the link to the form above.

The Origin

Generally speaking, this book is an extension of the Kings Island Park Hacks book. I, Mike, the creator and author, live near Kings Island in Cincinnati, Ohio. I saw the need and decided to collect and publish a guide filled with tips to help families deal with the challenges of the park. It felt good to share from my experience.

Following that first year of building a community and having dialogue via social media, I realized three things:

- The tips in the first book can be helpful for visitors to any amusement park, not just Kings Island.
- This 40 year old dad's individual perspective, even if helpful, wasn't enough for a wider audience.
- My long, personal stories were not as easy to search as well-organized tips, and a detailed table of contents.

In this edition, I've worked to improve those things. The scope of tips have been expanded to apply to visitors to any amusement park. All the amusement parks have similarities. We have studied many of them first-hand and have enlisted the community of readers and enthusiasts to help make sure what we write works for their home park.

I got some help. Krystal was a great help to me in launching the first Park Hacks book. She helped by sharing tips. She participated in the launch team. She also shared from her experience as a younger parent in her twenties with two young children. That was very different from mine, as a dad in my forties, visiting the parks with teenage kids. These combined perspectives make the book valuable for a wider audience.

Theme Parks v. Amusement Parks

To many people, these are synonyms. In this book, I'm intentionally separating more traditional amusement parks. Theme parks like Walt Disney World and the Universal Parks, are a different kind of resort experiences. There is overlap. The differences are becoming more blurred as amusement parks add more theming to their park sections, and theme parks feel pressure to add more thrill rides.

Look for future books that dig in more deeply to these other park or resort experiences, like Walt Disney World and Universal Studios.

Mike's Backstory

You can read the longer background and inspiration for the Park Hacks series on the About section of the Kings Island Park Hacks blog. In the spirit of this more focused, quick hitting guide, I'll give you the elements of my backstory that really matter when it comes to Park Hacks

I discovered the Steve Birnbaum's Official Guide to Walt Disney World, when I was a kid. It taught me tips and strategies for that park. Our family went there nearly every year. We also visited Cedar Point, Busch Gardens in Tampa, Geauga Lake in Aurora, Ohio and several others. I went on to write up multi-page guides for friends based on my experience. They returned enthusiastic about how the notes helped them to have a strategy to work through the park. They did everything they wanted and had time left over.

Now I live very close to Kings Island, near Cincinnati, Ohio. I've grown to know this park and its weekly and seasonal variations quite well. A year ago, while observing some very stressed families, kids screaming, I decided to write a guide. That idea became the 2017 Kings Island Park Hacks book.

Introduction | XVII

The ideas kept coming, both through comments with the audience and also as we had more experience. I also found another enthusiastic Park Hacker, and invited her to partner with me to develop that Kings Island book's next edition and this book, a book that shares similar tips that aren't specific to one park. We decided to point out ways to build similar strategies for whatever amusement park that you visit.

A few biographical notes about me. At the time of publishing, I'm 44 years old. I live in West Chester, Ohio with my wife Lesley and our three fun kids ages 15, 13 and 4. Besides writing about and enjoying amusement parks, I'm a multimedia expert, creative director, and digital marketing consultant in the Cincinnati and Dayton markets.

Krystal's Backstory

My background with Kings Island began in Spring of 1999. I was 8 years old when my obsession began for what, back then was called, Paramount's Kings Island. I had visited before then, but that is just from my parents' stories. I was in awe when I saw Kings Island and the campgrounds. I was fascinated by the sounds, smells, and sights. From then on, I made sure I knew everything that was going on at the park.

I got to know my husband at Kings Island. In the beginning of our relationship, it was *our thing*. After work, we would go to the park together. We got to know each other, more and more, as I talked his ear off about the history of the park.

Later, I had two little boys. I still went to the park, even while I was pregnant, because it was still fun, and relaxing. I am now raising my children to be future park hackers, like myself. It is an advantage, living close to the park. My children are toddlers, but they already know the park like the back of their hand.

In December of 2016, I met Mike Kunze. I was on Amazon, looking for Kings Island related things. I was having withdrawal, during the off season, missing being at the park. The Kings Island Park Hacks book popped up. With the knowledge I had, I was suspicious of the accuracy of the book. As I read the book on my Kindle, I realized I was not the only person who knew how to use the park's policies and procedures to my advantage. I submitted a Park Hack to Mike about locations of the baby changing stations. Let's face it, if you are a guy, that topic is probably not on your radar.

Mike and I continued to discuss the next year's edition of Kings Island Park Hacks. I jumped on board to help out and give the perspective of a young mother who has been a long-time veteran of the park. Mike came up with idea of extending the tips to a wider audience as Amusement Park Hacks. I am very excited to have helped him write it!

The Code of the Park Hackers

As we share these tips that long-time park experts have learned, it is important to make one thing clear. If a hack takes advantage of parks by teaching dishonest exploits or loopholes, then these books and blogs would not be helping the situation for the long-term.

The advice in the Park Hacks books is first for families who visit the park. We want them to have a better time. The park also benefits from the sharing of these tips, because these families will become happier customers. They gravitate toward visiting on slow days. They will also share tips and recommendations with others, growing new park customers. Over time, they will also spend more money, buying season passes and meal plans year after year.

Proper Line Position Shifts - Families or group of friends often want to ride together, on the same roller coaster train. Several times I've been asked if a friend can move in front of me so they can ride together. Families and groups with adults raised to understand fairness and politeness automatically do this the right way. They offer others to move forward to join their group. A position farther back is less valuable. It is not polite to ask people to move back a position to bring your group together. The way to do it, is to offer to others a chance to move in front of you, to even out your group. The person desiring the adjustment must move back, not forward. Certainly, people are reasonable and may hear your wish, and generously offer their position. These changes do not affect anyone further back, because two positions ahead of them are simply trading places.

Treat Park Employees with Respect - The staff of amusement parks can vary widely in terms of experience, attitude and work ethic. To be a good Park Hacker, you may encounter an employee that knows less than you do. Sometimes it is frustrating, but they are working in their job and hopefully improving in their skills. If you see something that is not as it should be, present your request to them in a reasonable and kind way, explaining the situation as clearly as possible. If that doesn't resolve your issue, you should back off and talk to a manager. Escalating the stress of the situation does no good for anybody.

I've had ride operators resemble Barney Fife while measuring my four-year-old, who had just reached the height to ride some new rides. She had the official bracelet and was good to ride one of these new coasters for the second or third time. Then an operator says he needs to check her height. I'm fine with it, she has her bracelet. Then for several minutes of the bar clearly brushing over her head, with contact, he explains that she's just not tall enough. I don't know what the issue was. I decided to swallow my indignation and return at a later time when he wasn't working that ride. Perhaps he got written up and was being extra careful. I'll never know. What I do know is that getting mad at this employee wasn't going to improve the situation. Most of the employees rotate, so just try again in a half-hour or later in the day.

Be Part of the Community - Park Hackers are a helpful community, eager to share tips and discoveries as they enjoy the park. We share ideas so we can learn from each other. From time to time we may ask an opinion. It will help everyone if, instead of liking or doing nothing, share your thoughts in the comments or Submit-a-Hack form. We want your input.

So many things boil down to the basic, golden rule, **Love Your Neighbor**.

How to Read This Book

This book can be read from cover to cover, if you enjoy perusing for strategies that you haven't considered. We've worked hard to keep the topics organized and the sections clearly marked so that you can drop straight to a section that addresses the problems you are experiencing or have experienced.

The book also represents the **http://amusement.parkhacks.com** blog and Facebook community that can be found **@amusementparkhacks** on Facebook. If you have a problem that isn't in the book, we invite you to ask us using the web.

If you have a Park Hack that helps you and your family and friends enjoy better amusement park visits, the best way to share them is using our **Share-a-Hack form**, **http://amusement.parkhacks.com/share-a-hack/**. Park Hacks featured in the book will earn you recognition in the next volume and a FREE paperback copy!

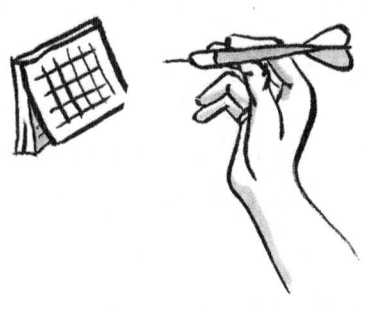

CHAPTER 1
PREPARE YOUR EXPECTATIONS

Getting Ready to Go

The tips and hacks in this book are designed to apply to any park, so once you've chosen a park that you want to visit, make sure you check the park's calendar. The goal of the Park Hacks is to help families have the best time at amusement parks. Your first step toward a good visit, is choosing to go on a day that is not crowded.

This first chapter of the book is about understanding the kinds of parks, the season during which you plan to visit, and considering the wishes of the different members of your family or group you intend to bring.

Annual Parks v. Seasonal Parks

There are a few details and patterns that differ between parks that operate year-round and those that are strictly seasonal. Annual parks never have a single time of the year when a majority of employees are brand new. Seasonal parks have a large percentage of workers who are brand new at the beginning of the season. Seasonal parks are only open for a portion of the year, for a specific number of operating days, a clear start and end to their season.

Parks that Operate Year Round

Amusement Parks in Southern parts of North America or indoor locations have mild winters that enable the park to stay open all through the year. Here are a few examples:

> **Six Flags Magic Mountain** in Valencia, California
> **Knott's Berry Farm** in Buena Park, California
> **Circus Circus Adventuredome** in Las Vegas, Nevada
> **Six Flags Over Texas** in Arlington, Texas
> **Busch Gardens** in Tampa, Florida
> **Nickelodeon Universe at the Mall of America** in Bloomington, Minnesota

Some of these have select holiday closures and others are open 365 days a year. Check each park's website for calendars and hours of operation.

Maintenance Schedules

Because these parks don't have an off season, each ride may be closed a few days a year for maintenance. If you have your heart set on a specific ride, it wouldn't hurt to check the park's website, fan blogs specific to that park, and even call the park's office before you go. That way you will be sure to have the latest information of any rides will be closed.

Annual Passes

If you're are planning to go a lot during the year, an annual pass for a park that operates year round can save a lot of money on admission. The date of you activate your pass usually sets the expiration to one year later.

Prepare Your Expectations | 3

With a good look at a calendar for this year and to this date next year, even if you live farther away, you can plan multiple visits to get the best value out of your pass.

Seasonal Trends

Annual Parks v. Seasonal Parks

Trends differ, Annual parks never have a time when so many employees are brand new the way a seasonal park does at the beginning of the season. Annual memberships can begin any time of the year. Seasonal parks have a specific number of operating days, a start and end to the season.

Seasonal Parks - North American Summer

Soft Opening - The park often opens back up following its dormant winter months. The maintenance and often new construction is completed and everyone is eager to see what is new. The weather might be cooler or even cold. Many park employees are inexperienced beginners, often in their first job anywhere. Expect ride operators and food services to not be running at an efficient pace. Once the initial excitement is over, there are usually light crowds. The first day of operation and weekends can get heavy and especially frustrating as employees learn their roles and start to pick up speed.

Most parks first start to operate on weekends and then will add weekday operation just before the Memorial Day holiday. Those weekdays before the main season are the best opportunities to visit the park with light crowds. Make sure you are prepared for shifting temperatures. It can be very cold, to very hot, even within in the same day.

Jean Lines from Columbus, Ohio shares this advice relating to the Spring Break season:

"If you're heading south to Florida for Spring Break, many parks, like

Six Flags over Georgia operate during Spring Break. Visiting an amusement park make a nice addition to a Spring Break trip. Remember it can get crowded on weekends, so if you can schedule your time there on a weekday, you'll find it a lot less crowded."

Memorial Day Weekend - This is the weekend that is trial by fire for the park employees. Hoards of people visit the park, and the operations can still be a little on the slow side. You won't catch me, Mike, in the park during this weekend. The only exceptions is if there is a storm predicted that clears up by the afternoon. Those can bring a surprisingly light day as people shift their plans to the other days of the weekend. If that happens, watch out. Those other days can be extremely heavy with double-sized crowds.

Once that holiday weekend ends, the employees are usually broken-in and moving very fast.

Summer, The Main Season - The majority of the operating calendar in North American amusement parks is between Memorial Day and Labor Day. Weekends are often heavy and weekdays significantly lighter. Some weekdays can get heavy. Tuesdays, Wednesdays and Thursdays are often the lightest, because many people like to extend their weekend in one direction or another.

If you're close enough, or have a schedule that is flexible enough to visit the park without a lot of advanced planning, following a morning or early afternoon storm makes for a great evening. Even on a rainy day, you can get a poncho or a raincoat and ride all afternoon and evening as long as there isn't lightning.

After Labor Day Weekend - Labor Day is the end of the main Summer season. It is usually another very heavy day, similar to Memorial Day. The main difference is that the staff is often running at their very best. Rides and food lines move swiftly.

Following this weekend, many of the regular Summer employees go back to school and college. There are other new hires or reassigned employees that may or may not be good at their new assignments.

The crowds on the remaining weekdays of operation are often very light and weekends can still be heavy to moderately-heavy.

Special Fall or Winter Events - We'll be talking about these later on in Chapter 7.

Check Park Hours

Always remember to check the park's operating hours for the day(s) you plan to visit. Sometimes the parks are closed to the public for private events. Weather considerations can also cause the park to close early. Do your homework.

If conditions change during the day, ask employees occasionally if there is any word if the park is closing early. Park staff communicate constantly, especially among the manager and lead positions. They can be an excellent source of information.

Setting Expectations

The best hacks that help you have a winning day, start by planning ahead. You can get lucky, flying by the seat of your pants. Life rarely turns out exactly as you hope.

Define Winning for Your Group

It is hard to get everyone's interests covered in a large family or group. Some want to try a new ride, others are only interested in a favorite classic. To win doesn't mean that someone else must lose. The objective is to consider everyone's priorities when planning.

For example, a young child may want to ride the same swing ride all afternoon. A teen might want to relax by the pool or get a rush on a thrill ride.

Older members of your group are also going to have a different idea of winning. Some of them may still enjoy a good thrill on a roller coaster. If they have back, leg, neck, or other health issues, they should use caution on some rides. Many of them have been enjoying the park for years, so make sure you listen to their stories about what the park was like in the past. Visits to the park with more extended family is a great time to slow down a little, enjoyed time together and build some memories.

The separate activities, like the ones that a young child can't participate in, don't have to fill the whole day. It is a good idea to ask and listen so that you understand what everyone cares about most. Work up a plan of times with the whole group doing some activities together and other times with separate areas of age-appropriate focus. With a little care try to ensure everyone in your group has a fun time.

Traveling

Depending on your distance from the park, the time you have available and your vehicle options you need to think about how you're getting to the park. The majority of people take their personal vehicle. If you have reason, like a larger group or a vehicle reliability challenge, you may decide to rent a car. The serious roller coaster enthusiast may also decide to fly to try the new ride at a park on the other side of the country.

If driving a long way, make sure you have a plan for entertaining your passengers. My (Krystal's) children are used to looking out the windows for their traveling entertainment. It may not be a bad idea to invest in a portable DVD player. Teens, more than likely they will be talking, texting, or playing games on their phones. If you have them, don't forget to bring along the external batteries or car chargers so that phones don't die when you need them to communicate within the park.

If you're staying at a hotel near the park, make sure you ask about a

Visiting Alone

There was a time when I (Krystal) frequently went to the amusement park as a single person. Visiting by yourself can be exciting or depressing. When you go, there will be couples everywhere. Sometimes even sporting matching "His and Her" shirts, to emphasize they aren't there alone. If you are single, don't forget that you have the ability to do whatever activities in the park that you want to do. You can determine what "winning" means for you. If you want to roam aimlessly around the park, taking in the atmosphere and do some people watching, you can! You can also bounce to whatever rides you desire. This is a good chance to focus on doing what you want. You may even be paired up with another single rider and could hit it off. Getting a new friend is a great souvenir.

Alternate Plans

Bad weather can happen anytime and anywhere. So have a backup plan. Locals have an easier time being able to find something else to do, because they know the nearby area. If you're going to sit out a storm, ask the park employees about nearby malls or fun shopping opportunities. If the storm looks like it will last more than an hour or two, it is better than sitting in your car waiting for the weather to clear. Make sure you get your hand stamped.

So if you are a local, and the weather is not working out as you hoped, this might also be a chance to visit that cafe or shop you've been meaning to check out. You could also use that time to get some errands done. It can help pass time, and keep your day from being wasted.

For a traveler, it is a little more difficult. You may want to go back to your hotel room or campsite to read a book or watch some TV. One of my (Krystal's) favorite things to do at times like this is to drive around and grab a bite at a local diner, or go see a show. You don't have to give up the chance of exploring a new location just because the weather is not perfect.

What to Bring

If your park is seasonal, Summer is when most of the visits will occur. If that is the case, make sure you are prepared for heat and sun. Make sure you have comfortable shoes or sandals. Flip-flops can work if you are used to walking long distances in them. Short-sleeved or sleeveless shirts, ball caps and, of course, sunscreen are also essential.

Don't forget that weather can and does change. Keep an eye on the forecast, even a day or two before you go. The temperatures can shift quickly in a lot of the country. It is a good idea to have a change of clothes and a jacket in the car. You don't have to carry it around with you, but a walk to the parking lot is easier on your wallet compared to buying dry clothing at the park. I (Krystal) go by the saying, "Hope for the best, prepare for the worst." When I visit my home park (Kings Island) I make sure to have an emergency kit in my vehicle that includes a spare change of clothes for each member of my family.

Versatile clothing works best when you want to adjust, rather than doing a full change of clothing. Windbreakers are great. Not only do they keep your skin warm when it's windy, but it can also works as a rain coat. Tear away sweat pants are a choice that is certainly versatile, just make sure you have shorts on underneath. Pants that zip at the knee, can turn into shorts.

If it is very rainy, you might be able to still have a fun day with a rain poncho or an umbrella.

A small backpack or a drawstring bag is great for stowing these items until you need them.

Prepare Your Expectations | 9

Many other park experts advise visitors to travel light and deal with things as you come. Certainly there is a possibility to overpack. Here is a list of other useful things that you might consider having with you, at least in the car.

- An extra towel
- Extra bathing suits
- An extra pillow
- Allow your children to pack a couple favorite shirts
- Battery pack, phone power boost. Solar versions are also available.

How do I, Krystal, carry all this stuff around the park? My personal favorite option is a fanny pack. Yes, I have been teased for it. It helped me to be hands free, with no stress on my shoulders. I had the three things I needs, wallet, keys, and phone.

Stroller - I, Mike, have shared this tip on the blog and in the previous book. I consider this one of the best Park Hacks. If you like to keep a few items with you, like a refillable cup, a jacket, and even a camera, it will be hard to enjoy the thrill rides properly. Those of us who bring small children know that a stroller is a great traveling home base. It is a seat where your kid or kids can rest their feet or take full unconscious naps.

The stroller also offers you a fairly safe place to stash your stuff that is cheaper and more convenient than getting a paid locker. I've heard of organized thieves snagging high-end strollers from Walt Disney World, but a basic, inexpensive stroller is usually ignored and not a temptation for thieves.

One of the bits of advice I offer to readers of the Park Hacks books is that you can take these tips as far as you want. I encourage park visitors to maximize their fun and money savings, even if it means being a little weird. I've mentioned that a good Park Hacker will stop before it crosses the line of breaking rules or cheating, but if you want to try what I,

Mike, refer to as Extreme Park Hacks, you go ahead and be weird like me!

Extreme Park Hack - Bring a stroller to use as we've described, even if you don't have a kid with you! It is like your traveling cart where you can keep all your stuff. There are a couple cautions. Strollers are often safely parked around the kid-friendly attractions. Employees and park visitors don't usually bother them. There is no guarantee it will not be rummaged or taken, but in our culture, it is far safer a platform to keep your belongings, than just leaving them in a pile on the ground or sitting on a table. The areas where there are no kiddie rides, is generally not a safe place to leave a stroller. There is safety in numbers and you can leave a stroller for a while and return to it later.

Preparing for Rain

You don't have to let rain spoil your whole day. We mentioned being prepared with a poncho or an umbrella. Ponchos, which are great if you want to ride rides.

Let's consider your feet. Wet socks in shoes are unpleasant and cause blisters on the feet. Water shoes are my choice if it is going to rain or if I plan to do water rides.

Last pointer (and maybe you've covered it or are going too). Only carry what you need! Your backpack with the change of clothes and the kitchen sink is going to cost you time and money. There is a reason the newer rides don't have bins for loose articles. Capacity. So all those backpacks, drink cups, stuffed animals, basketballs and purses either end up in a filthy unsecured bin (park is not liable for items in the bins) or in a secured bin you have to rent. Eliminate the headache and Leave it in your car and get it later or if you must a small fanny pack.

More Helpful Hacks

Have each person in your group make a bucket list for the visit! Put the most important items at the top of the list. Throughout the day, compare lists to figure out the best way to help your group hit their top priorities.

CHAPTER 2
TICKET AND PASS OPTIONS

Tickets

The variety of ticket options can be surprising. There are also many places to get tickets. You can buy one pass for one day right at the ticket window by the park entrance. With a little research, local businesses, like grocery stores will also sell you passes, sometimes at a discount. You might also get store shopper card points for your purchase. Do some Google searches on "Cheap tickets for [the park you plan to visit]," to gather your options.

There are many people who only get one day to visit a park during a season. Distance, work and school schedules, and other activities may dictate that visiting a certain amusement park is only a one-time thing for the season. As far as Park Hacks go, this is the most expensive cost for a single day. It also puts all the pressure of having a fun visit on the one day you have selected. Make sure you've considered the calendar date with regard to the part of the season you're in. Aim for a weekday, if possible.

If that one day has to count, you should also keep an eye on the weather and plan to arrive at least a half-hour before the gates open. You want to get to your priority attractions right away.

Multi-day

Some parks sell multiple-day passes. If you're traveling to the area, having a second day to see what you missed, may be worth the expense of a hotel. The ticket cost is usually a good deal less than buying a single-day ticket twice. Even if you have an obligation in the middle of a multiple-day ticket, it may still be a good value with a full day skipped.

Krystal's Thoughts:
With multi-day tickets, planning to divide the park in half will help you focus on quality time. If the park has a waterpark, spending a generous part of one day there, so you have a chance to enjoy that environment.

It is a good idea to vary the ride experiences. After you do a ride that gives you that Adrenaline rush, then go to a gentler ride or one with short line. It will give your body time to settle down ensuring you don't get sick, which would limit the quantity of rides you feel like doing.

Season Passes

The parks often offer a variety of season pass options. At our home park, Kings Island, they incentivise you to get your season pass early by offering the special Gold Pass. That option is only available from the pre-season through about the Memorial Day weekend. After that date, you can still get the common season pass. But it doesn't have the added perks, like free parking, food and merchandise discounts, early access to the park and Extended Ride Times (ERT) for certain rides, etc. Make sure you read all the options to see if your park has a special pass. If you go several times, just the cost of parking can really add up.

Most Six Flags parks also offer a Gold Pass which includes free parking. You'll also get VIP entry into the park and an extra Bring-A-Friend Free ticket.

Cedar Fair Platinum Pass - This is the Cedar Fair pass that is an upgrade over the Gold Pass referred to earlier. It gets you admission into all Cedar Fair parks.

Six Flags Season Pass - As of this writing, it appears that a season pass for Six Flags gets you admission into all 13 Six Flags parks.

I repeat this as a mantra for the Park Hacks series. Rules and options often change, even mid season! Sometimes options enjoyed by the visitors disappear and other times very exciting bonus options appear without warning. Park management is constantly tweaking and managing how the park operates. They want to make sure the most people have fun while also keeping the park profitable. If you're a season passholder, just make sure you are prepared for changes in schedules, ride and restaurant offerings and other park features.

A season pass can be a large investment for a family, especially a large family. If you do your research and a little math, you can see how many visits would be the equivalent if you paid every time. It is often about two visits to break even. But that is missing one of the best things about the season passes. What a season pass gets you is the more opportunities, so that you can relax during each visit. You immediately get to concentrate on what you want to do and how your group is feeling. It is much easier to enjoy a half-hour sitting on a bench in the shade (or in the sun) while you take in the atmosphere and ambiance. You don't have to stress about how much you have to accomplish on that visit.

It is the effect it has on you that is the best benefit. Visits to the park are on your terms, without pressure. If your schedule allows you to plan a surprise afternoon, following a thunderstorm. Your family can often enjoy a park with the crowds washed away. These can be the absolute best impromptu visits to the park.

Annual Passes

If you're are planning to go a lot during the year, an annual pass for a park that operates year round can save a lot of money on admission. The date you activate your pass usually sets the expiration to one year later.

With a good look at a calendar comparing this year and through this date next year, even if you live farther away, you can arrange multiple visits to get the best value out of your pass.

Season or Annual Pass Discounts

It is easy to forget that your pass almost always gets you a discount on the purchase of items around the park. When in doubt, hand the cashier your pass whenever you buy something. If you purchase items online, like tickets for other people, you can look for a place to enter your pass ID number. This often works for food, souvenirs, special events, premium ride experiences that cost extra. Always ask if your season or annual pass gets you a discount on a purchase.

Special Food Tickets

If you are planning to visit for one full day, you may find special ticket deals that include meals with your single-day admission. Make sure you do the math and read the fine print. Sometimes you're paying the same as two average meal prices for two meals. You'd be better off buying what you want. Plus, it will limit your options. It is an amusement park day, you may want to get a bucket of popcorn or a funnel cake as your meal. It isn't a healthiest choice, but is not an option that is usually allowed as a meal. Some passes will let you get several meals through the day, like one every 90 minutes. If you anticipate eating a lot or if you plan to split or alternate meals with another family member, this could be a really good bargain.

All-Season Meal Plans - Some parks sell a ticket upgrade that gets you meals all season long. If you live close enough, having a meal becomes an excuse to visit the park right alongside the desire to see a show or ride a certain ride.

Make sure you read the details and the list of meal options that are available. The options can change mid-season. You also might have picky eaters in your group. If your child only eats pizza, they might get tired of visiting the park for the purpose of having a meal, because they aren't open to the variety of options.

Some families buy meal plans strategically to split the high-calorie meals among more family members. The parks are getting better at limiting this. The person the pass is attached to, must have entered the park. They usually don't require the photo match the person buying, because families often split up to hold tables or to get drinks.

Our family, which includes two adults and three children get along pretty well on three all-season meal plans. If we had more, we would probably gain a great deal of weight. It is a good value, but make sure you keep in mind that the park food is generally very high in calories.

Fast Pass

Some parks sell or offer a pass that gives you access to a shorter line. There are a variety of ways these work across different parks. The Disney theme parks were some of the first to offer their Fastpass system. I, Mike, have used Disney's version, and am still not a fan. It makes the lines far longer for those who don't have a Fastpass. The value it adds in the big picture, is a level of gamification and interaction to the park experience. People spend a lot of time calculating and reserving fast pass access for the rides that are their highest priority. It also allows a mechanism for the park to offer VIP, or line jumping access to anyone as a perk or as a benefit to offset some inconvenience. The final result is that I end up going on fewer rides over all. Two or three have shorter waits and the rest far longer.

Ticket and Pass Options | 17

The way this kind of pass works is more just. They are not bought or sold. They simply are a way to give priority access to those who care and take the time to declare one or two top priority rides. Visitors can get easier access to a limited number of rides of their choosing.

The majority of amusement parks, now have different similar Fast-pass-style upgrades. I'm an opinionated guy and consider some forms of these passes to be immoral. We were raised to see cutting in line, as a rule that was not to be broken. It is based on fair play. In other parts of society, paying money to get around an offence of society is frowned upon. I'm surprised more people don't jeer and yell at people who pass by in these special lanes. But I also want to be clear, it isn't really the people who buy them that has me worked up. It is the park management that I have a problem with. By offering these, they are reducing the quality of a general ticket. So it is in jest that I suggest we call out the "cutters." I'm hoping through the book to offer strategies that are so valuable, that you will never need a pass like these.

The Six Flags parks have a FLASH Pass. The base level of this pass isn't a bad idea. For a price, you forgo the requirement of standing in line. You're still forced to wait the same amount of time, but technically you're not cutting. This makes the lines appear shorter. It also is great for the park, because it gives visitors more opportunity to shop or eat when they would otherwise be waiting in the queue. Their pass allows for groups of up to six to share one pass and return like they would at a restaurant when their table is ready.

There are two upgrades to these FLASH Passes that start to get into the problem of buying your way in front of other people. The Gold and Platinum version cut your wait time to get called back to the ride for a higher fee. That means for the extra money, you are cutting in front of other people. That gets a big thumbs-down from me.

The worst of these I've experienced is at the Cedar Fair parks. The Fast Lane passes, for a one time price, allow you to cut in front of all the lines, all day. This is the peak of immoral line cutting. The park is allowing you to buy your permission to line jump, something that used to get you ejected from the park.

I enjoy laughing at those who use these when the lines are already very short, which is most days that I go. They've paid money and not gotten much value. The other times, when the crowd is very heavy, the Fast Pass lines are often long anyway. On days when the park's offer Fast Lane passes as a perk of renewing season passes, they are practically worthless, because everyone has one and the lines are short on the days when they let you use them.

It is my hope and prediction that these passes are removed in a few years. In the grand scheme of things, they are a gimmick the park uses to get money out of people who are looking for a chance to buy their way to a position of higher importance over other park visitors. If you want to be one of the more extreme Park Hackers, join me in yelling "cutter!" whenever they walk past you. We can shame this option away, if we work together.

Krystal's Thoughts:
As a Park Hacker, I do side with Mike on this subject... to a point. My husband and I have a tradition of going opening day without our kids. On that day, we get the Fast Lane pass. We aren't looking for special treatment, but to ensure that get to ride everything. The rest of the season, we will have our toddlers with us. In my opinion, if you get these passes because it is the only day of the season you get time for yourself, go for it!

If you buy it on a day where the regular lines are already short, then you have just wasted a lot of money! With Cedar Fair adding an all-season Fast Lane upgrade for season passes, it will be hard to get a good value. On all but the busiest days, you're only going to benefit from using them on a couple rides with long lines. Those aren't cheap, so make your purchases wisely.

Food

A day at the amusement park is often not a normal day for eating typical meals. Many visitors get up very early and drive an hour or two to get to the park. If you stayed at a hotel, maybe you had a continental breakfast or a breakfast at a restaurant. You will also walk more.

So to take advantage of some of these tips, you may have to plan ahead and intentionally shift the time you would normally have a meal. Doing the things that don't come naturally is one of the core advantages of being a Park Hacker. The key theme here is to not do what everyone else is doing.

Park Food is Expensive

Amusement parks are not known for fine cuisine. Sometimes the food products can be quite tasty. The fact that visitors are a captive audience, and the restaurants are staffed by many young, immature, inexperienced employees with little sense of cleanliness and customer service, the experience sometimes can be unpleasant.

There are strategies that can help you enjoy better quality food, eat healthier and save time waiting in long lines, and spending tons of money.

The meals are often very high in calories and typically loaded with carbs. Sugar, bread, corn and potatoes make up a big portion of the fuel to sustain you during your visit to an amusement park.

Ordering a whole pizza, or splitting a meal entree are two options to cut down on the costs. A whole pizza often costs about the same as two meals, but it can feed three or four people. If a couple of friends partner up and spit an entree they can cut a sandwich in half. Many items are served with a mountain of fries that would be formidable for any one person to eat alone.

Long Food Lines

If you can successfully shift your eating schedule off of the normal times, you will be able to avoid the majority of the crowds.

Some parks open just a little ahead of lunchtime. If you decide to eat your first meal soon after you arrive, one strategy would be to walk quickly to any restaurants at the back of the park. The crowds will be very light there because most people hit rides first thing. The negative side to this strategy is that you will lose valuable ride time right at park opening.

There is a similar strategy to moving back toward the front of the park when most people are further in the park. Crowds tend to spread pretty evenly, but if you pay attention, you can sometimes notice that one area is particularly heavy. For instance, the area with the kiddie rides usually has a higher than average portion of the crowd.

Snacks

Read the park policy on the website to see what their policy is on bringing food in from the outside. Most parks do not allow food to be brought in. If you have very small children, family members with allergies, or a nursing mother in your group, you can often get permission to bring in special food.

There is nothing the park can do to prevent you from keeping snacks in the car. One member of your group can walk to the car and your group can get a hand stamp to step outside the gate for a packed snack.

Refillable Snacks - This is no longer available in my home park, but some parks may still offer a refillable popcorn bucket. In the past, I've seen it treated like the soft-drink option where you pay $1 for refills after the day of purchase. Keep your eyes open, there are sometimes seasonal treats like this too. This winter during our home park's Christmas event, I've heard there will be a refillable hot chocolate plan!

Packing Your Own, BYO, or Tailgating

I've seen families set up elaborate tailgate food spreads in the parking lot. They surround the back of a minivan or hatchback with lawn chairs and enjoy a value-priced feast just a few steps outside the park.

If you're driving several hours, you could plan a stop at a grocery near the park. You can use Google Maps and search, "groceries near [the park you plan to visit]." The tool will highlight supermarkets in the vicinity. Many of them will also sell ice, even dry ice, and foam coolers to keep your food fresh until lunch.

Healthy Eating v. Fuel

Most parks are offering healthier options on their menus. Sometimes, they are unfortunately not the items that are offered on the meal plans. Read the menus for special options like salads or pizzas with gluten-free crusts.

Meal Plans and Special Deals

If you visit the park frequently, there is no better deal than an all-season meal plan. The parks are betting that the majority of families only come a few times and enjoy the convenience of not worrying about food. This is an especially good for families that use the park as the babysitter for their teens and pre-teens during the summer. With a meal plan on their pass, they can get dropped off early in the morning and picked up again in the evening knowing their kid will be fed during the day.

You need to look at the food options to see if the restaurant and items allowed on the plan are selections that you'd like to eat, more than once, during the season.

You should also pay attention to any time restrictions on the plan. On the plan that I, Mike, use, you can get two meals during a day. They have to be spaced four hours apart.

If you're not a frequent park visitor, some parks will also sell you a special ticket with some meals included. Some have one meal included, which is good for parents who can't trust their kids with cash. Other plans enable you to eat many meals through the day, often 90 minutes apart.

Watch for other park-specific details. At Six Flags parks, if you get an all-season meal plan, you get a refillable drink cup included with your food plan! At Cedar Fair parks, drinks are not included with the meal plan meals. You can either ask for water or a refillable drink plan to pair with your meal plan. Cash (non-meal-plan) customers usually do get drinks included when ordering a meal.

Refillable Drink Plans

Some parks sell a couple of souvenir cup options. Others sell a pass to get fresh paper cups during the length of time you are in the park. Still other parks, like Holiday World in Santa Claus Indiana offer free drinks all day, included with your admission! Explore the options and any limitations in the fine print. Some parks may have a time limit on how often you can refill.

All-season options have a few variations. There often is a higher-priced cup that has refills all season for no additional charge. Another option may include free refills on the day of purchase and then charge a nominal amount (typically $1) for refills on a later visit.

There are also plans that are attached to your season admission pass that get you paper cup drinks any time. It is like the plastic souvenir cup, but you don't have to keep track of a plastic bottle. I'm surprised I haven't heard anyone sensitive to environmental issues raising a fuss. At my home park, there are no cup lids or straws, so keep that in mind. If you want to carry it around and sip from a straw, you'll want to go with the plastic cup.

Another consideration is that during peak times and late in the day, the drinks stations are often in disrepair. Some have missing nozzles and others are just out of ice or flavors. Be prepared to walk along to the next refill option if you are picky about your drink.

After several hours of consuming soft-drinks, a person starts to feel kind of gross. One park hack that I've observed surprisingly few times, is to fill your souvenir cup with ice water or the filtered bottle fill stations at the drinking fountains. The days when I make sure I'm well-hydrated, I feel great a lot longer than the rest of my group.

External Dining Options

If you are visiting a park in a town you don't know well, you can do some research before you go to learn what outside restaurants are nearby. If you use Google Maps and start where the park is, you can widen your view to include any neighboring towns. Then type "restaurant" or "food" into the search bar. Or in fewer steps, start with a search "restaurants near [the name of the park]." That will fill the map with markers for all the restaurants nearby that are noted on Google Maps. Sometimes a restaurant is not recorded correctly, so you can use the Street View tool to virtually move up and down those streets to get a reasonable idea of the food options that the streets nearby will offer.

With the knowledge of what is a few minutes away, you can extend the dining options. You will have to make sure that everyone gets their hands stamped before exiting. It is also a good time to change socks or adjust your wardrobe layers, if needed.

If the park is crowded, you might even be able to eat more quickly than you would have in the park. It will also likely save you some money. But consider that against time outside the park and the gas to get there. Also, ask an employee to make sure you can get back into the parking lot with your receipt from earlier. If you have to pay an additional parking fee, it will absorb all that money you tried to save.

Leaving the park for a portion of the day will also be an idea covered in the strategies for breaking up a long day. You can effectively kill two birds with one stone if you visit a mall or a special site near the park.

For instance, a lot of people travel over an hour to visit an IKEA store if they don't happen to live near one. Near Kings Island, there is an IKEA about fifteen minutes away. You can get lunch and take a long air conditioned stroll through their fun store.

CHAPTER 3
RESEARCH THE PARK

Parking

When I, Krystal, go to my home park there are two sweet spots that I try to hit. One is a shop that sells turtle caramel apples, literally called "The Sweet Spot." The other is an area of the parking lot that I prefer. It is my parking lot sweet spot!

Having a good spot in the lot can have several benefits. Mine is not the closest to the entrance. It is actually a little bit closer to the exit, and a little far from the crowded parts.

I see the headache guests goes through to get a close parking spot. But at my "sweet spot" I have more room to open my doors wide to get situated. Plus, there is hardly anyone else who parks there, so my vehicle is easy to find. I have fewer worries about my vehicle being dinged. I can park, and walk in worry free!

There is no reason to park close. You are going to be walking a lot inside, give yourself a less headache when leaving. You can be in front of the crowd when you exit. You won't have to squeeze in-between cars. I get anxiety when driving, especially when there are a lot of people around.

Another reason I like my special area, is that at the edges of the lot, there are no lines. The rows end up being less tidy, but the other drivers tend to allow more space between cars.

Mike's thoughts:
I agree with so much of what Krystal has described here. I want my experience in the lot to be hassle free. I don't want to have kids climbing all over my car. I try to swoop around the hustle and bustle of families getting out of their cars by parking beyond them. I also don't mind walking a couple extra rows. I see people waste a lot of time trying to get into very full sections, looking for a gem of a place that an earlier visitor left open.

I only play that game well after the park has opened. If the park has been open long enough that there isn't a lot of activity and some families may have begin to leave after a morning visit, then I try to spot, or have spotters look down the row for gaps as we drive by the lot on the main road. Some parks aren't going to have good visibility for this, but if you can see ahead that there are some gaps in a close area, it is a big help.

If you look at a satellite view of the parking lot, compare the distance of the most distant places to the entrance gate. It usually is a shorter distance than you think. Compare it to walking between two distant attractions in the park. It isn't worth it to lament a distant parking place.

One thing to make sure you do, is to take careful note where you parked. Unless you have a special place like Krystal described, this can also be a problem for frequent visitors. I've had many times when I've gone several days in a row. It is easy to get confused. "Did I park in this row today, or was that yesterday?" The problem is real. I like to text the row and side to my wife so we both have a reference to where the car is. Sometimes we drive separately, meeting at the park. I'll text, "row 38 on the far side" because each row number has a side close to the entrance and the far side.

You can have the row number and still waste time walking in the wrong lot aisle, because it is on the other side of that row. So take careful note, every time!

Nathan Endsley from Marion, Ohio shares that most amusement parks have a smartphone app. Many have a feature where you can pin your location on the app when you get out of your car. At the end of the day it can give you directions back to your car.

Following Nathan's great tip, Krystal and I talked about it. She has had experience with park apps getting buggy and unreliable. Make sure you have some practical idea of where you park. Don't trust it to be 100% reliable. If the app is working well, it can be a great help, but I like keep things in my head. It helps me to be able to use the knowledge when unexpected opportunities arise.

The Map

Amusement parks are complicated places. Many have developed over decades, so the layout may not always be intuitive. Ideally, there is a plan that is easy to walk, where you'll find all the attractions you want at a natural flow. But life isn't often ideal.

Using the map of the park well is one of the most valuable Park Hacks. You will learn how to steer clear of crowds if they are not balanced around the park. You will also be able to cover more of the park because you will not be wasting time and effort meandering and recrossing your steps.

Get the Map in Your Head

You can usually download the official park map from their website. When you decide you're going to a park that is new to you, it is a good idea to find that digital map and start looking at it. Pay attention to the position of the parking lot and the front gate. Then try to get the general idea of the park firmly implanted in your head.

You will likely have a map with you on the day of your visit, but having a general layout in your head will be a big help. You will think about what is near you for a more strategic choice for what to do next.

Park Regions

If you are just getting acquainted with a new park, most parks give you a shorthand method for understanding the layout. When you look at the map, hold it farther back and take it in more generally. Do you see different themed sections of the park? Is there an area where most of the kiddie rides are collected? Is there a water park? Is there an area that is themed more historical or to the American West? There could also be a classic midway where most of the games are organized.

Some parks might organize based on the theme of the entire park. Holiday World is a great example of this. The areas are organized around specific holidays. There is a patriotic area themed as Independence Day or 4th of July. There is a spooky area for Halloween. Of course, being located in Santa Claus, Indiana, there is a major section dedicated to Christmas.

If you don't have time to memorize the entire map, at least take note of where each of these regions are. It can help you navigate with more clarity. You will be way ahead of the families that try to see the whole park by randomness or simply walking toward what they see next.

Landmarks

Walt Disney pioneered a lot of innovative ideas when he designed Disneyland. He wanted the areas of the park to visually draw you forward. Many cartoons depict a horse with a carrot dangled in front of them or a dog with a hot dog. Walt, using the hot dog concept, called these visual enticements "weenies." As you enter the gates of the Magic Kingdom, the castle is the weenie that pulls you along Main Street. The other lands surround the central hub. Each of them has a "weenie" that you see in the distance. By allowing yourself to pursue things that you see that interests you, you should be able to see everything. That strategy, however isn't the most strategic method for working through a park.

An amusement park has an additional advantage for navigating a park. Roller coasters, drop towers and other tall structures can help you quickly orient yourself in an unfamiliar park. In Kings Island, there are three towers that are about 300 feet tall. Those are great reference points for anyone who wants to figure out where they are.

Meeting Places

If you're traveling in a group or with enough family that you will split up for a time, you should always clearly discuss meeting places. Cell phones are a big help, but picking out high-visibility, locations where your group can gather is also necessary.

Make sure the spot is unique and be specific. For instance, don't say "I'll meet you by the pizza restaurant" only to find that there are three separate places that offer pizza. An unusual feature, like an unusual statue, the entrance or exit of a specific ride, or the base of one of the park's major landmarks, are all good choices.

If you have a large group and are choosing where everyone will gather at the end of the day, you can choose a store that will contain those who have arrived. It is tempting to wander off again.

Transportation

Most of the transportation within an amusement park is on foot. You will be doing a lot of walking. In some parks, there are different transportation options. You might be able to hop on a tram, a train, or even a cable car. Sometimes people see these options as a ride experience, but occasionally you can take advantage of their ability to move you to another area of the park while you rest your feet.

Divide and Conquer

One of the best time savers, is to concentrate on one area of the park at a time. It is easy to waste your time, and your energy bouncing back-and-forth across the park, pursuing every whim. Instead, stick to one region of the park and try to do everything that interests you there before moving on.

If you find an area to be too crowded, you can always skip it and plan to return to that section. It is a lot easier to keep track of an area that you wish to revisit than an individual ride.

Rides

The most prominent activities in an amusement park are the rides. In a later chapter, we will get into different types of rides and how to enjoy each of them to the fullest. Here we want to prepare for your visit with a base of knowledge for the rides. If you know what your family can ride and have a good idea of what interests you, you are more likely to leave satisfied that you concentrated on activities that you wanted to do.

If you have small children, or a physical limitation, like being pregnant, back problems or a heart condition, there are some rides you can cross off your list at the start. The park's official website lists details about each ride, including height limitations and warnings about the physical dangers.

If your child is very close to a height threshold, choose carefully the shoes that they wear the day of your visit. A nice, comfortable pair of sneakers and socks will protect their feet from all that walking, but also may unlock access to a half-dozen rides that they wouldn't be able to do if they wore sandals or flip-flops.

Shows and Live Entertainment

I have always had a particular interest in rides. It is hard to get me,

Mike, to stop to watch a parade or a fireworks display. I want to take advantage of those moments to hit the rides when fewer people are in line.

In recent years, I've opened up my thinking to discover that some of the live shows are really enjoyable. Most parks have some kind of live performance. Sometimes they are ensembles of performers that move through the park, popping up for a short performance in the streets. Other parks have multiple venues for music, stunts, acrobatics and magic shows. Check the listings for what is available on the day you visit and choose a time slot that fits as you plan how you will work through the park. The performances have set schedules. Make sure you take note if the day of your visit is an off-day.

If you are a regular visitor, make an effort to see the shows several times. My family enjoyed our park's acrobatic show and saw it several dozen times through the season. My point is, that for live shows, it is never exactly the same show twice. The more you see it, the better it gets. You will get to know the performers and will start to spot more subtle variations and improvisations that the performers add in.

There are many benefits to learning to enjoy the live programs. You develop an appreciation for the performers and their art form. You get a few minutes to rest your feet, sometimes even in an indoor, temperature-controlled theater.

Park Policies

Dress Codes

You should review each park's policy on dress code, to save yourself a hassle, if you think you may push the boundaries. There are often rules clearly posted and enforced at amusement park water parks. You are also usually expected to wear t-shirts, tank tops and shorts at the minimum in the park. I've heard that people who walk over from the waterpark are told they must cover swimsuit tops or bottoms before they are allowed on rides. So be prepared to adjust your attire as you transition back to the park.

The swimwear you purchase that you intend to wear to the waterpark should also free from metal rivets or parts of any kind. The metal parts cause scratches and grooves in the slide plastic and fiberglass material. You may be offered a choice by a water slide attendant. You can exit the ride or let them modify it for you using a pair of scissors. The choice is up to you.

Weather Patterns

Each region has its own weather personality. If you get to know how weather tends to move through the area where your park is located, you can judge if a storm will pass in time to allow for a fun visit.

I, Krystal, am a fanatic for weather, especially storms. Where I live the best strong storms often go right around us, which is upsetting.

Using weather.com (The Weather Channel) or Accuweather, you can get some good information.

Using those apps, you can expand the radar map to see all the storms that may affect your day at the park. You can check regularly to be aware if a storm has built up or if it is losing strength. Look for the animated map option. Take note of the wind direction and how fast it is moving. You can get a feel for if, and when, that big blob of rain will hit the park.

I have been at a park when bad weather was about to strike. I check the radar on my phone. It helps to see more current information on how bad it is likely to get. We can decide if our family should wait it out.

Most parks shut down outdoor attractions when lightning strikes within a 15-20 mile radius of the park. This distance ensures that the ride operators can get everyone off the ride. It also gives guests the opportunity to move to a safe spot. While the storm is rolling through, most, if not all, indoor live shows will usually still go on as scheduled.

During this time you can shop, catch a show or get a bite to eat. The park employees have been working hard to enforce the rule to not run in the park. This is especially important when the ground is wet and visibility is poor. (However, if a tornado is coming, then I, Krystal, am running.)

If it's raining with lightning, and you have children, get them under cover. It is a nice time to visit a store or restaurant. You could also go to your vehicle. You can decide to leaving for a while, intending to return. (Get your hand stamped.) You also have the option to hang out in your car, play a game or take a little nap.

If there is not lightning, many of the rides will go on operating in the rain. We mentioned in the section about packing your gear, that a poncho can come in handy. These or a nice hooded raincoat or windbreaker can protect you and make the wet day into a great chance to hit the rides faster than any fast pass.

For the Park Hacker, the best thing about a little bad weather, is that it drives heavy crowds away. If you spot a rainy day that will clear out by late afternoon or early evening, those have often been the absolute best times we've ever had at the park.

Cameras and Drones

Remote-controlled quadcopters, often referred to as drones are a recent issue. Most, if not all, parks have rules prohibiting these. If you are not an authorized professional operator, hired or invited to use them at the park, do not bring them in. You should also not fly them near the park. There are many safety risks. Just leave them at home.

Parks have also started restricting the use of cameras of any kind on rides. It is usually stated to be a safety consideration. A poorly managed cell phone could easily slip from a rider's hands, striking a rider sitting behind them. The park has to draw the line somewhere. I've heard stories of recent years where a person has been permanently banned from the park with no refund for filming during a ride.

There are professionals with special camera rigs that can be firmly attached to the rides. The park has their own media staff and there are press events that may allow filming. If you want to see video of a particular ride, a quick search on YouTube will usually bring success.

CHAPTER 4
FAMILY AND GROUP MANAGEMENT

Letting Kids Explore

There is an opportunity at amusement parks to help your kids to grow in a reasonably safe and contained public environment. You can watch for opportunities to give them a chance to do something alone, while you watch from a safe distance. Have them go get napkins, or ketchup. If they have a friend or sibling the right age, you can have the pair go on their own to ride while you sit near the exit. It is a nice way to introduce independence.

Quiz Your Kids

You can learn a lot about your child's personality and ability to handle responsibility. I, Krystal, already test my three- and four-year old toddlers on their awareness of their location and geography. I believe that by starting my children at this young age to be aware of their surroundings, it will improve their safety.

This goes right along with the previous map topic. My kids love looking at the map of our home park. Every time we go, they must get a copy of the map. Then, while we visit, I allow my children to direct us where we are going. They can lead us to where we will eat and rides that they want to try next. I will also change the game up by having them direct me to a ride I want to ride. Doing this with me, shows me that they are aware of what is going on. Even when you have a map, it is a benefit to know in your brain where you are.

A way to test older kids, is to have them meet you somewhere. You can note how long it takes them to get to you. If they don't show up quickly, two things may have happened, you find them in a different location from the one you said, or they took a long way to get to you because of an inefficient path or their wandering attention.

With experience you can begin to know about how long it takes a person or a group to move from one spot in the park to another, even by going different routes.

The main reason of these fun tests, is to prepare them for an emergency or to protect them from ever feeling lost in the park. If something bad were to happen and they did not have time to take their phone out or stop to look at the map, they will instinctively know where to go.

Your kids may surprise you with their capability. Test them out and then decide for yourself how often to let them go on their own.

Family Locator App

I, Krystal, have a Sprint phone and I use its family locator app. The Sprint Family Locator allows anyone on the plan to locate any other person on their plan. It is not always 100% accurate. I have had it locate me at one place. Then moments later, relocate me in another part of the state, all while I was standing still, nowhere near either of those two markers. The technology isn't perfect, but is helpful. Having Wi-Fi on

helps with pinpointing. If the other person's phone is not in a location where data is being used, or the phone is off, the app won't locate it.

Smartphones and Wi-Fi Communication

Kids today are often carrying powerful, and expensive, devices in their pockets. This additional method of communication makes it far easier to keep your group in touch if it separates for a temporary activity. A quick note before you load onto a roller coaster, will help the others know when you're nearly done. That gives everyone else a chance to either state where they are, or begin moving toward the exit of your ride.

The use of texting by phone becomes increasingly helpful for check-ins as the distance between you and your kids increases. If your kids are mature enough to go a more extended time on their own, you may even drop them off to be picked up later. A good flow of communication can help make the pickup rendezvous go smoothly.

This gradual extension of freedom is a nice way to teach responsibility and to instill the confidence that your child can handle themselves on their own.

Baby Swap

Nathan Endsley reminded me of a feature for families with very small children who still want to ride the thrill rides. Each park may have a slightly different policy for how you use this benefit. Check the website or ask a ride attendant.

The idea is that the group only waits in line once, but the party can split into two groups so someone can attend to the young child while the others ride. Then one adult swaps places to allow the initial baby-watcher to ride.

The execution is often operated using their fast pass system so that the second group can bypass the line. This is a nice benefit for families where both parents might enjoy a ride on the same thrill ride. If it is a new policy or not frequently used, I've found that park visitors may have to inform ride operators what they intend to do. Other parks may have the concept well established.

Cedar Fair parks have a Parent Swap sheet that you can get at Guest Relations. It lets your Group 2 riders, the ones first minding the baby, enter the ride through the exit. Group 1 riders wait in the line. Group 1 rides. The baby passes to Group 1 after they exit, and Group 2 then rides. Different parks and different rides may not all follow the same procedure. It might be worth stopping and asking the attendants near the ride entrance to be sure how it works.

Some parks, allow children, who are too small, to wait with parents in line. Then, when it is time to ride, they pass through the train and wait by exit, or in a kiddie corral. The kids may not be directly supervised, but they are generally safe for the minute or two while the others ride.

Graduating to New Heights

It is an exciting time in a child's life when they grow tall enough to ride a ride that they previously weren't tall enough to ride. It can be a fun opportunity to mark the occasion with a celebration.

If your children are picky eaters, like mine, use their height to your advantage. I (Krystal) tell my kids if they want to ride the bigger roller coasters they have to eat their food so they can grow.

Notes from Mike:
Your height can vary during the day. You're taller in the morning and then your spine compresses as you walk around. It is more obvious in taller people, but it is in your interest to get an official measurement with a bracelet or ID card as early in the day as possible.

If your child is close to that measurement threshold, be careful about changing shoes or hairstyle, they might not meet the same height requirement on a different day. That could be frustrating.

Small Adjustments

Shoe lifts, hairstyles, cowboy boots, other thick-soled sneakers are a few of the methods you can use to help a child that is nearly to a height threshold. It is a good idea to give these kids a pep talk to prepare them for being rejected from the ride. Some ride operators are more picky than others.

There also needs to be a voice who advocates for the ride operators. One of our insiders reminds us that operators are trying to do their job consistently. The stick is a quick reference, but the official scale stand is the true measurement. Every kid that is close, is going to be checked. A wristband may help them not be re-checked as cautiously, but they can still be measured on the stand.

Not measuring carefully is putting their job at risk. So remember to hold your temper if someone judges to be more cautious. People are human and kids sometimes stand up straight, and sometimes they don't. So if you know your kid measures up, I say calmly back off and try again later! Employees rotate positions on a regular interval, like every hour.

If your child is too short, they are too short. Don't berate, threaten or try to beg the employee. Even if they've ridden before. And please, don't yell at your kid. One operator told me, "I've seen it more than a few times."

ID Cards and Wristbands

Some amusement parks offer ID cards with the child's photo and height printed on it. There is a good and bad side to these cards. The good, is you can show the card without having to get measured each visit. They will get the wristband that is indicated on the card. The bad side of the card, if your child grows during the season you will have to purchase a new one. Last check they were about $12-15. Getting a card might be a fun celebration of the new achieved height. But you can also save the money and just have them measured each time you go. I (Krystal) buy IDs for my kids each year, but that is more as a keepsake for our memories.

If your child is close to the margin, it is in their interest to get measured early in the day if the park offers wristbands. This helps, but does not guarantee, that they will not have to stress about being re-measured each time they go on a ride.

Activity Changes

We've mentioned the benefits of breaking up a long day at the park for different activities. You can leave the park for lunch, or head to your car or hotel for a nap to help keep the fun going into the late hours. If exhaustion sets in and tempers flare, then you will be forced to prematurely cut your big day at the park short.

If the park has a waterpark that is included as part of your admission, that is another break option that provides an extreme change of activity, a change to use different muscles. If the day is hot, it is an opportunity to cool off. The lounge chairs and umbrellas may also give you a great chance to take a short nap that is more comfortable than your car.

Special Treat or Snack Time

The time at an amusement park can be a physical drain. Small children are especially prone to a lapse in energy or getting hungry before a mealtime. If you are on the frugal side, you can take a short walk out to the car to enjoy a packed treat. A small cooler in the car can keep fruit, granola bars or other treats at a good temperature, even if the car gets hot.

If you have budgeted a certain amount of fun money, you can break up a time between meals for a refreshment. It is a good way to spend time when the rides might be at their most crowded. Enjoying a special ice cream treat, funnel cake or container of popcorn might be as memorable a moment for your family as any of the rides.

One year at a park in Florida, we shared two luxurious brownie sundaes among our five family members. By splitting, it wasn't so much food that we went into a food coma, and it was also cheaper. We had a fun moment enjoying a nice treat before continuing on a long, hot day at the park.

Another note on splitting. Krystal has shared on our blogs that she has a special favorite, a turtle candied apple. These are huge and luxurious apples, covered in chocolate, nuts and caramel. Krystal mentioned that you can ask the people at the counter to cut it up for you. There will be less waste and you could more easily share the decadent treat among several people.

Midway Games

Going to a park can be all fun and games until you become agitated by losing so much money playing games or realizing that your vehicle can't seat your passengers plus the abnormally large plush animal prize you finally won. Do not fret, these tips can help you get fun from the midway games at the park.

Most of the games are skill-based and not a science. Of course, they are not setup to make it easy to win. Unless you are very lucky, you will have to rely on skill and a perfect performance to win.

The Rope Ladder is best for those who have good balance. The trick is to move like a cat, slow and graceful. Move opposite limbs at the same time. Your left hand, moves forward at the same time as your right foot. You can also spread your body out, like the poles held by a tight rope walker. It help your stability more than trying to stay close to the center.

High Striker, also known as a Strength Tester, or The Strongman Game, is where you bring a hammer down on a pad that launches a projectile up toward a bell. Just about everyone thinks it's about strength, but it is really about applying the pressure right to the center of the drum you hit.

My (Krystal's) favorite game is the **popping the balloons with darts**. I learned quickly a technique to pop all three balloons. First, if the wind is blowing, avoid the game. Your target can move right as you throw. Also, make sure the board you're throwing at is filled with balloons. Wait until the operator replaces any missing ones. It maximizes your chances. The last hack for this game, is to throw the dart hard! The dart is not sharp, if it is a light throw it can bounce the balloon or glide right by it.

Once you have won your game, congratulations! Now, what are you going to do with your prize? I like to wait until late in the day to play, so I don't have to worry about getting lockers or carrying a big stuffed animal or other prize around with you. Another thing you might want to think about is if your vehicle has the space to bring it home. People often fail to think ahead about the challenge transporting their prize. The smaller items are easier to carry, plus if you have little ones, it can help keep them entertained while waiting in lines.

The main point of the games is to have fun! If your park makes you get gaming cards, keep them with you, whether you win prize tickets or not. The cards collect points which add up to tickets, so don't throw them away. I have multiple cards and save them until the end of the season. I am often surprised by how many points or tickets I have accumulated.

Shopping for Souvenirs

It is fun to bring home a souvenir. Rather than getting tons of little knick-knacks, I (Mike) am an avid coffee drinker, so I like to occasionally get a special mug to commemorate special vacations. When I'm at my home park, I look at all the stores and still have never been tempted to buy anything. I'm very picky about the mugs that I get. But having one category, then I feel like it is OK to check out all the stores in pursuit of something I like. These typically aren't things you're buying for their usefulness, but to help maintain a memory of the visit.

Watch for sales. Amusement parks often offer close-out pricing on items to clear shelf space for something new that is coming. One doesn't often consider getting a bargain at an amusement park, but if it is something you like and the price is agreeable, enjoy the discovery!

Krystal's Thoughts:
I consider myself an avid coffee drinker like Mike, but I am huge on getting coffee cups of different size and colors. At my home park, I always get one regular mug and one travel mug that are themed to the park. I also agree with Mike on watching for sales. I recently got a puzzle featuring the park's railroad. It was originally $8, and I got it for $1. (I've been working on that puzzle for the past 4 months now!) I am big on wearing park-themed gear, but only if I can get it an a good price.

Handling Problems

Problems happen. We've covered different ways you can deal with bad weather. Some challenges can be avoided with some good planning and a careful monitoring of the condition of your group.

Kid Melt-down Tantrums

If you are visiting the park with small children, you can improve your chances of success by keeping them fed and rested. The tips we've shared for dividing the day into chunks with different activities is very applicable here.

Little kids don't have the energy capacity and reserves that grown-ups have. They also react to their physical condition with less control by their intellect. Meaning, an adult can recognize they are hungry or tired and choose to take care of it. A small child often starts screaming or acting out when they feel bad.

If you intentionally squeeze more variety into the day, you can avoid the shoe-throwing, foot-stomping, pink faced melt-down that is easy to observe near any park exit around dinner time. I always feel sad for the families who are dealing with an overtired kid. The parents often are tired and frazzled themselves.

Following a good hour to 90-minutes of rides in the kiddie area, it is a good idea to shift to a show or a longer, calm activity. A ride on a train that lasts 15-20 minutes or a 25-minute show can give the little ones a chance to recharge their batteries. The late morning might also be a great time to consider an early lunch, which helps avoid the main lunch rush and keeps the kids energy stabilized.

If it is a very hot day, plan a calm and cool activity for the hottest part of the afternoon. If there is a dark ride, an indoor show, or a wooded path or playground to explore, these can help the kids avoid that dinner time melt down. If you have a stroller, try to set the seat back to a recline and encourage some rest. A kid who has had a full morning and afternoon at a park will often conk out for a fully unconscious nap.

We've also mentioned that if a water park is accessible, or a hotel with a pool or an air conditioned room, a short time away from the main park can help protect the quality of the later evening. This investment of down-time can help the kids reach the end of day fireworks display in a good mood.

Baby Problems

Krystal shared this as her first Park Hack in the 2017 Kings Island Park Hacks book. Baby changing tables are available in nearly all restrooms. That includes both the Women's and the Men's Rooms. Don't let the dads skip their duty.

There are also multiple family restrooms now that have additional space for accessing strollers, and diaper bags. You also have the benefit of corralling toddlers in a safe environment while you change a baby or use the facilities yourself.

Most parks have a special child-care facility, including a place for children to wait for their lost parents to find them. It should show prominently on a map and will likely be near the kiddie area, first-aid station or a visitor services counter.

Messy Problems

This might be a baby-caused issue, a nausea-caused issue, or whatever. If you have gotten yourself into a mess, you might be able to take advantage of the park's facilities for just such a problem. If you ask the staff, they may have showers and even laundry facilities available to help you get straightened back out. One of our focus-group participants shared this special information. I, Mike, had no idea this was an option at any park. That is an impressive level of customer service.

Mechanical Problems

Rides are generally very safe. Safety procedures also help make sure they stay that way. If a warning happens for the ride operator, like a small element signals an error, the ride can come to a sudden halt. There are stories all the time about people being stuck on a ride, waiting for the maintenance to get it moving, or worse, waiting for a long ladder to be brought in to help you safely exit a hard to reach part of a ride.

The fact that the park is set up to keep you safe, more than just comfortable, leads me to a personal rule. Before you get on a ride, make sure you've used the bathroom! I've been fortunate, by never being stuck for more than a couple minutes on the hill of a roller coaster. I know Krystal got stuck for around fifteen minutes recently due to a power outage. I have heard of riders getting trapped in a ride for two to four hours.

To make it worse, I often enjoy my souvenir drinks quite a bit while visiting. So the drink and restroom visit cycle is pretty regular for me. It would be very embarrassing to get stuck for a time longer than my bladder could hold out. So I keep that rule as often as I can. Go before you... (ahem) go!

Crowd Problems

Walk Away

If the crowds get too heavy and you have the freedom to try the park another day, sometimes it is better to drive on and skip the park. Once year on Memorial Day I thought I'd pop over to my home park to see what it was like. I knew it would be bad, but was still surprised. Since I had a pass that included parking, all my experiment cost me was some time. The lot was so congested, that it took almost 40 minutes just to drive back out the exit!

I understand if you're making a special trip and have limited time to make your visit. Then you don't have that option to simply skip the visit that day.

That is one of the best benefits of being close and having that season pass. If it looks crazy busy, you don't feel the pressure to go in, or to stay if conditions get too unpleasant for other reasons as well.

Check Other Areas

One would think that crowds even out around the park as the crowds build up. A heavy day is usually busy everywhere. But sometimes, for different reasons, the crowd is very uneven. If the demographics are predominantly families with little kids, that can make the kiddie area really crowded and leave surprisingly short lines on the thrill rides. The opposite can also happen, the thrill rides may be heavy, while the kiddie rides are light.

If the weather is very hot, more may flock to the waterpark and if it is on the cool and cloudy side, you may have the waterpark to yourself.

People Watching

If all your options are exhausted and you are in a park with really long lines and nothing else to do, you can enjoy the interesting people. The park atmosphere is another draw for those who love amusement parks. There are many times when my family goes to the park and hardly does anything. We walk the park, enjoying the sights and sounds. So don't get down if you don't have the opportunity to ride every ride. Much of your pleasure of your visit can be gained by having the right attitude.

When I'm away from a favorite park, there are only a few of the rides that I long to ride. The main thing I miss is that opportunity of just being there!

Large Groups

I got a lot of experience in my youth going to parks with my church youth group. We would have a bunch of about 60 people and visit Cedar Point. Most group leaders are great at organizing and keeping up with stragglers.

The methods I saw that worked well, was to have an adult or older kid be a leader of a small cluster of kids. It is nice if the total number of the group is even, so that no one has to ride alone. You can coach the group leader to make sure that everyone rotates so that everyone feels included.

The group leaders should make sure that their group does not divide up. They are also the primary contact for the group, keeping some communication with the main leader. A hierarchy of leadership can help keep the chaos organized.

Helping the Loners

Sometimes kids in a large group wander off and sit, sulking rather than riding. There are ways to make sure they feel included, they can be assigned a role of being an ambassador to the different groups and move from cluster to cluster.

If it is just a phase they are in, you can let them sit and sulk but give them instructions for reporting their condition and location to the leader periodically.

Meal Times

Using a meal, like lunchtime to guide the entire group toward a mandatory check-in, you just need to tell them that everyone must show up at a certain time and place.

Work Team Building

Most parks are eager to sell to groups. Businesses can provide a special event for their employees by setting up an outing to the park. Check the park's website for group sales. If your employer needs a nudge that the employees would like that better than a membership to a fruit of the month club, you can contact send the contact information to your company's activities planning leaders. The park's sales representatives will reach out to them with enthusiasm.

There is a lot of flexibility among the options for a group. The company can pay for all or part of the ticket cost. They can provide a catered meal or just have meal vouchers attached to the passes. It is a nice perk to provide that doesn't cost as much as many corporate events.

There is another benefit. The relationship dynamics change when you're riding with your work friends. What may have been a team of friendly colleagues, holding themselves at a typical arms-length distance, can become a lot closer of a friendship when they hear one another squealing like a little girl on a roller coaster! It is a fun way that a business can reduce attrition and build a strong team.

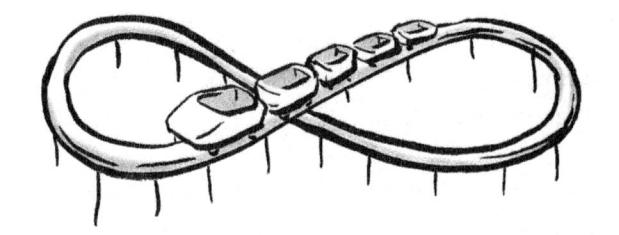

CHAPTER 5
RIDES

Thrill Rides

Thrill rides are the main attraction for most amusement parks. They offer a range of sensations and physical forces. There is often the psychological thrill of heights, anticipation, darkness or special imagery to add to the experience. This guide is being designed to be useful to visitors to parks everywhere so we will not concentrate much on specific rides, rather we'll review different types of rides, styles of roller coasters and when meaningful, their manufacturers.

There are groups of roller coaster enthusiasts who know all these manufacturers and can identify them be a section of track. I, Mike, have always loved roller coasters, but hadn't previously gone that deep. The communities on the web have inspired me to learn more and I'll share a little information here. This is not an exhaustive list. By doing Google searches and reading each manufacturer's site, Wikipedia, and other enthusiast sites, you can go far deeper and search for the creators of the rides at your home park. Having this information opens up fun ways to find rides that are similar to those that are already your favorites.

Ride Manufacturers

Bolliger & Mabillard, or **B&M** makes large, smooth, highly-engineered roller coasters, often inverted or wing coasters.
www.bolliger-mabillard.com

Intamin makes a wide variety of styles, and is especially known for giga-coasters, water rides, and drop tower style rides.
www.intaminworldwide.com

Rocky Mountain Construction is known for large, complicated roller coaster constructions. Most recently they made the news for Cedar Point's transformation of Mean Streak, an extremely large wooden coaster, into Steel Vengeance, a large steel track using much of the existing wooden support. **www.rockymtnconstruction.com**

Arrow Dynamics has been around a long time. They are now owned by S&S, below. But if you've ridden The Matterhorn, Pirates of the Caribbean or Mr. Toad's Wild Ride, you've been on some of their more famous older attractions. They also build log flumes and classic inversion coasters like Cedar Point's Corkscrew and Kings Island's Vortex.

S&S is the company that bought Arrow Dynamics, and is now the creator of a wide variety of unusual and technically challenging thrill rides.
www.engineeringexcitement.com

Vekoma makes roller coasters with innovative designs. The three that I know are all very fun, but they share a trait of very slow-moving lines, because of complicated loading processes and mechanisms.
www.vekoma.com

Mack Rides is another manufacturer with a wide range. They offer innovative roller coasters, water rides and dark rides. **mack-rides.com**

Gerstlauer a German designer of roller coasters, both steel and wooden.

They also offer giant wheel designs. **www.gerstlauer-rides.de**

Schwarzkopf is another German manufacturer that created roller coasters between 1964 and 1983. **schwarzkopf-coaster.net**

Maurer Söhne a German engineering company that makes highly technical steel coasters and giant Ferris wheels. **www.maurer.eu/en.html**

Great Coasters International is a roller coaster manufacturer who has been in the news a lot for elevating wooden coasters to its new modern level. The recent Mystic Timbers at Kings Island and Gold Striker at California's Great America are good examples of the fast, lively and surprisingly smooth motion that can now be achieved by a well-designed wooden coaster. They also created their Millennium Flyer articulated trains to run on these active, twisting track designs. **www.greatcoasters.com**

D. H. Morgan Manufacturing or **Morgan**, now owned by Chance Rides, was originally founded by the son of the founder of Arrow. It still offers a wide range of roller coasters, giant wheels, dark ride systems and people movers. **www.chancerides.com**

The Gravity Group is another manufacturer of modern wooden coasters, featuring their own high performance Timberliner trains to ride on them. **thegravitygroup.com**

Premier Rides manufactures highly-technical and richly themed steel roller coasters. Many of them feature LSM launch systems. **premier-rides.com**

Zamperla is a manufacturer of highly-themed carnival-style theme park rides. Many of the rides in your park's kiddie area, may have come from them. **www.zamperla.com**

Philadelphia Toboggan Company has been making amusement park rides for over one hundred years. They have manufactured many classic

carousels, wooden roller coasters, and roller coaster trains, and other technological advancements.
www.philadelphiatoboggancoastersinc.com

Dinn Corporation was a designer of roller coasters for a brief time in the 1980s and 1990s. The founder was Charles Dinn, the head of construction on The Beast at Kings Island. The Dinn company designed, constructed or moved several large wooden roller coasters.

Custom Coasters International was founded by Charles Dinn's daughter after Dinn Corporation closed. They specialized in wooden roller coasters. It operated from 1991 to 2002.

Dynamic Structure, now **Dynamic Attractions** is the manufacturer of rides that use special innovative effects like robot arms and 3D glasses.
www.dynamicattractions.com

Roller Coaster Corporation of America (RCCA) from 1979 to 2005 created several large wooden roller coasters. Son of Beast was one of them and noteworthy because it was a wooden coaster hypercoaster, which also had a loop.

Giovanola, based in Switzerland, was a manufacturing company with a very long history, going back to 1888. In the late 1990s it became a subcontractor to Intamin and from 1998 to 2001 was designing and building their own roller coasters. The company went bankrupt in 2004.

That is a fairly complete list of roller coaster manufacturers. I, Mike, am not an expert, but I enjoyed spending some time researching and building this solid list including some of the characteristics. If I've left one off that you'd like to see included, please let me know using the Park Hacks, **Share-a-Hack form.**

It is fun to read a list of the rides at my home park and learning which ones are siblings from the same manufacturer. In the next section we'll also see how some rides from certain manufacturers influence the way the seats work. This may be valuable if you have discomfort on rides or find a hard time fitting in seats because of a tall or large stature.

Physical Challenges

Every thrill ride has a warning sign posted near the entrance that clearly posts the health risks and types of physical strain you may experience.

One ride operator I talked to had a lot to say about helping people fit into rides and enhancing their safety and comfort.

Disabilities

If you have a disability let the guest services know. They give you a green or white sheet allowing you to come up the exit rather than maneuvering through the line. The ride associate gives you a time to return, as if waiting the amount of time you'd be in line, then you can board immediately. These passes are good for up to four guests. Even if you have a condition that would normally prevent you from riding, sometimes you can still ride. There may be special harnesses available for riders who may be amputees or have trouble using the restraints the way they were designed for the general public.

Large Riders

People come in all shapes and sizes. I, Krystal, have experienced issues with height on rides. We hear a lot about minimum height requirements, but rarely consider the max. The max height requirement is because of overhead obstacles. My husband stands at 6' 4". We've had to deal with this issue many times.

If you are a tall person, struggling to latch your over the shoulder restraint, you can try slouching. Bringing your butt toward the front of the seat and hunch your shoulders down. It might help. Don't get discouraged if you don't fit. Some rides have a test seat out front. If you are larger than average, either by weight, height or both, it might help save you the frustration of wasting time waiting in line or being very uncomfortable.

On typical rides with lap bars this tip is a little different. You will want to sit in the middle or last seat of your car. When you get in, you will want to tuck your feet under the seat in front you and cross your ankles, this helps to lower your legs for a better, more comfortable fit.

Some rides have special seats that are larger or have longer seatbelts. Ask the greeter or operators before you get in line. They may direct you to certain rows that are better able to accommodate your need. Employees will try everything in their power to help people squeeze into a seat or restraint. Sometimes it just doesn't work.

Referring back to the ride manufacturers, classic rides by Arrow and most wooden coasters are designed to be a lot more capable for larger guests than the Intamin or B&M rides.

Here are a few more quick pointers, shared by an operator, to help ensure comfort and success:

- Empty your pockets. A wallet or a phone takes up space and can make a difference.
- Press your butt all the way into the seat, and sit up straight.
- Suck in your stomach as much as possible, while the restraint is being set.
- Ladies, to fit better on rides with over the shoulder restraints, press *the girls* together!

Being Trapped

Earlier, in the Mechanical Problems section, I mentioned it was a good idea to use the restroom before riding. There is a possibility that you may have an extended wait if the ride were to experience a malfunction. So do all you can to make sure you are comfortable in your seat, you

Introduction | 55

never know if you might have to stay in that position for a while.

Special Modifications

There are adjustments you can make to your own ride experience. The experience and sensation on some rides change quite a bit depending on where you are sitting. If you are worried that you will suffer from motion sickness, you will want to aim for the middle of the ride. This is especially true on swinging boat rides, and the roller coasters with the longer trains.

VARIATIONS IN SEATING

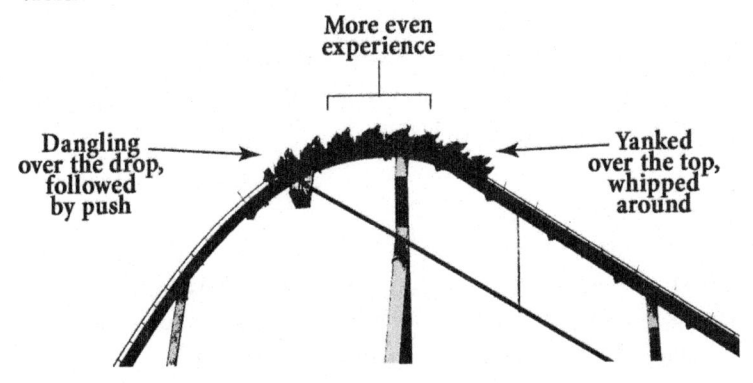

More even experience

Dangling over the drop, followed by push

Yanked over the top, whipped around

Front Seats - There are more extreme sensations in the front and back of a long train. If you look at the photos, the front of the car dangles over the crest of the hill, while the middle and rear of the train completes its climb. Then there is a tremendous sensation of being pushed down the hill as the rest of the train's weight starts its descent. There is also an added psychological thrill of looking down the hill, suspended, waiting in anticipation of that fall.

Rear Seats - The back of a long train or the outer edges of a swinging ride, also get more extreme motion changes. As the train reaches the top of the hill, rather than feeling suspended, the sensation is more of being yanked up and over the top of the lift hill. The tail of a long train feels more like you are being whipped around with each turn.

Wide Rides - If your train of vehicle is four or six seats wide, you can also enhance or reduce the sensation by moving to the edges or the middle of the seats. If a four-seat inverted roller coaster goes into a barrel roll, the outer seats make a wider circle. The middle seats will be fun, but slightly more neutral.

We'll talk about these variations a little more for people who have ridden a bunch and need ways to shake up their experience.

Avoiding Discomfort

Whether you are hoping to avoid a negative physical reaction or are hoping to repair the damage already done, there are some things you can do to make the situation better.

Nausea

Smile! - If you think you're going to throw up, or feel strong nausea coming on, you can improve your chance of keeping your composure by grinning. That's right, smile a big tooth-showing smile.

This funny Park Hack was inspired an episode of the original CSI (Vegas) television program. The character, Sara, was working on a particularly gross crime scene and she looks up with a big, Cheshire Cat grin. It was intended to seem out of place. When asked, she went on to explain that the big smile helps control the gag reflex.

I've tried this and have had great success. There may be a doctor who can explain why this happens, but it may be one of those mysteries of life. Like how saying the words "peanut butter" out loud, immediately shuts down the feeling you are about to sneeze.

Blacking Out or Passing Out

I love aviation. I, Mike, briefly studied to be a pilot a few years back. This tip is something I learned while watching documentaries about fighter pilots and aerobatic pilots.

If you're abdomen feels bad from too much jiggling, or if you feel like you might pass out at any point during a ride, flex your abdominal muscles hard! Tightening down your stomach muscles is one of the ways these pilots manage the effects of extreme g-forces.

This has worked for me. I use this during the fast-launch roller coasters like Kings Island's Backlot Stunt Coaster, and to a lesser degree Flight of Fear. These two rides have the Linear Synchronous Motor (LSM) launch at the start. It occasionally makes me, and others I know, start to black out. Since I've been using this abdominal flex technique, I've had no problems.

I briefly mentioned back in the section on refillable drinks that there are great advantages of staying properly hydrated, with water. There is also the added benefit of staying well-hydrated, is that it improves your ability to avoid blackout! By stopping more often for a drink of water, you're improving your ability to ride lots of rides without feeling bad. Even without a refillable cup, you can request water cups at any restaurant or drink stand. Water fountains and bottle refill stations are also helpful.

Joint or Back Pain

When you're in a particularly aggressive ride that is turning hard or rattling your body a lot, you can save your head, inner-ear and spine some of the rough usage by actively riding the ride. Think of a bobsled team hurtling down the run at the Winter Olympics. Those skilled athletes shift their weight and angle their head with every turn. Horse riders also actively move in rhythm with and counter to the horse's motion to maintain comfort and control while on the moving seat.

When I say to ride actively, I need to be clear that you also should not to brace yourself, tensing against the ride forces. That will hurt you. Keep a little tension, but allow your body to flex and flow with the ride's motion. It is kind of like when you have to stand a long time and people tell you to not lock your knees. You can maintain a slight muscle tension that helps resist damage.

This is not official medical advice. I'm not a doctor. I'm a dad, in my 40s, who likes to ride lots of rides with his kids. Using these techniques has improved my ability to ride more than two major thrill rides in a day. That used to be my limit.

Categories of Rides

Family Rides

Amusement parks offer a variety of rides suitable people of all ages and sizes. From the carousel, to a swinging ship, the selection of rides are designed to give amusement to everyone. By choosing wisely, there are good sequences for introducing rides to children. The kiddie rides often don't move much and have the shortest lines. Even riding while a parent watches can be scary enough for a small child, so take your time.

If you have an infant, there are some rides where an adult can accompany the child. Rides like the carousel, or the train, offer bench seating that will be some of the first rides your child remembers.

Dark Rides

Rides come in many styles, sometimes there is overlap, too. But the rides that are more about experiencing a story by passing through scenes with special visual effects and lighting, these are the dark rides. Some thrill rides have components of dark rides, but usually these are not focused on fast motion.

I, Mike, grew up going to both Walt Disney World and Cedar Point. In the 1970s - 1980s, there were several great examples of classic dark rides around. Unfortunately, old classic dark rides have been disappearing. Modern ones are nice too, but the quirky, sometimes horrific imagery in the old dark rides actually held a charm and nostalgia.

Cedar Point had Earthquake and The Pirate Ride for many years. These had creepy depictions of gore and hangings, illuminated by blacklight.

In Walt Disney World, the dark rides had a range from the simple and fun Mr. Toad's Wild Ride, up to the richly themed and elaborate Pirates of the Caribbean and Haunted Mansion.

Today, many amusement parks have one obligatory dark ride. In four of the Cedar Fair parks, there are version of Boo Blasters on Boo Hill, which is a reskin of the Hanna Barbera Scooby Doo ride. The ride is light and fun with a few chills for the smaller riders. They also have an interactive component where you shoot ghost targets with your Boo Blaster gun.

Holiday World has a very pleasant Thanksgiving-themed ride that involves shooting targets, not with a gun but with a themed turkey call.

There are many documentaries available on cable and the Internet about dark rides. The large theme parks have gone larger in scale with Hollywood movie-themed rides and Disney's Indiana Jones Temple of the Forbidden Eye and Dinosaur rides.

I have many opinions about dark rides, wishing parks would put more energy into the more classic versions of these ride options. They sometimes have complex ride systems, like Disney's Peter Pan's Flight where you are suspended above a miniature London and Never-Neverland. These rides are a great contrast to the outdoor thrill rides and can often be a nice break for your feet and a chance to cool off.

Spinning and Swinging Rides

Physical forces don't only come in the linear kind like roller coasters. Some rides like the traditional Scrambler or Monster rides spin you around and pull you abruptly in different directions. These often make people feel ill. Try to hit them at times not immediately before or after you eat.

There are other, larger-scale spinning rides, like the large pendulum rides. Some of these also get up to a fast linear speed as the rotation compounds with the swinging motion. These rides can goof up your inner-ear if you do too many rides in a row. It might be a good idea to spread out the most intense rides. The cumulative effect might wreck half your day, leaving you groaning and stretched out on a bench.

The fun thing about these rides is that they are sometimes good rides for grown-ups and small children to ride together. The forces are also less violent as some of the more rattly roller coasters.

If you're looking for a gentler experience, some of the rides that rotate or swing have inner and outer seat options. Aim for the seats more toward the center. The outer seats move through a more extreme path. Other rides treat all riders the same. You also want the larger riders on the outside of any rotation, in case the rotation causes riders to slide outward. A larger rider might unintentionally squish the smaller one.

Tall Rides

There are a set of attractions that offer the best views and the most pleasant, gentle rides in the park. There is just one catch, they do it high above the ground. If you're not afraid of heights, these drop towers and tall spinning swing rides are great fun.

If you don't like heights, there is not much I can do to force you to try them. I'll encourage you to try going up on the taller rides, and gradually taking in the elevated position. The lift hills of roller coasters, may be tolerable. Instead of closing your eyes, looking as you gradually climb may help condition a tolerance for heights. Look down, look back behind you, and riding in the back seat and looking back at the empty track as you ascend, are fun ways to spend the climb.

If the park has an observation tower, or a sky bucket ride, you can use that to expose yourself to heights. Don't let it upset you, if you want to overcome this phobia, take it slow and look for opportunities to practice.

For me, a guy who has no fear of heights, I see how the structures are stable. I understand that my being up there doesn't make any significant difference to the weight on the ride. Objectively comparing being on a solid platform, is not different than being on the ground, helps me not fear the fact that I'm high above the ground. It is a mental game. I believe, if you desire to win it, there are ways to get up there comfortably.

CHAPTER 6
LIVE ENTERTAINMENT

Acrobatic Shows

Each park offers their own selection of shows. Several Cedar Fair parks have acrobatic shows created by a company called **Haut Vol** (**www.productionshautvol.com** "haut vol" is French for "top flight"). They are headquartered in Quebec, Canada. This company creates richly-themed acrobatic programs, combined with fun visuals and music.

If you've seen a Cirque du Soleil presentation, you're in the right ballpark. In fact, by following some of the performers, I know that several of them work with Cirque du Soleil when they get the opportunity. The amusement park shows are simply smaller scale.

The shows are fun and entertaining, but the real magic happens when you are able to see the show multiple times. When you get to know the performers and the performance, a level of fun opens up as you learn to appreciate the subtlety. The performers do the show three or four times a day, six days a week. Sometimes they get hurt. Sometimes things don't go quite right. There are also times when they all have their act working great and they each push to do something a little more amazing than normal. It is the way they adapt, adjust the program and communicate immediate adjustments to one another that takes the viewing experience to the next level.

The performers also embellish the show as the season goes on. The first couple weeks are performed straight, as written. Everyone gradually gets to know how the parts of the show work together. Later, the silly improvisations start to show up. It is subtle, a person seeing it for their second or third time wouldn't spot the change. It is such a treat to experience the casts' inside jokes with them.

Get your seat early, at least thirty minutes before the showtime, to make sure you get in. Go as often as you can. The experience gets better and more interesting every time!

Stage Shows

If you like pop music or retro, tribute performances look for the musical shows that may be available the day of your visit. Every show has an off-day, so make sure you check if that is a special interest of yours.

There is a similar progression of development among the cast in the musical stage shows. Some of the cast are highly experienced and well on their way to being superstars. Others are very new, maybe just on stage with an audience for the first time since a ballet recital.

If you like to interact, sit toward the front, at the edges of the rows. It is common for the performers to take off among the crowd. You may get a high-five!

Street Performances

A special, often unexpected, treat for those who are wandering the park. Some amusement parks have special performances from visiting groups. Others have regular performers who pop-up in different areas of the park to put on special performances.

One great example of this was at Holiday World. They had a group of singers and dancers who appeared in the different themed areas. In the patriotic Independence Day themed area, they had prop rifles for maneuvers and twirling routines. They sang patriotic songs about America. Later, you could spot several of those same performers in the Halloween area for a series of spooky, fun songs themed to that holiday. It is an efficient use of performers to use them throughout the park, just changing the theme of their costume and music to match the area.

Character Meet and Greet

Kids love to meet characters. This is not just true for their favorite costumed cartoon character, but also the performers. Many kids get excited about the idea of meeting a character. When the moment finally comes, sometimes it is fun and sometimes it can be scary. I have seen kids cry and hit at the characters to get away. I've also seen kids run up to them for a big hug.

Live performers are a different experience. They come out at the end of their show. Sometimes it's the whole cast, and sometimes it is only a few. It is nice, even for adults to go up and talk with the cast. You can ask questions about how long they trained, or what inspired them to pursue this as a career.

Many of them travel from across the country, or even around the world. Others are local talent. They are usually nice, and willing to answer any question you have. Be prepared for the occasional language barrier. This is also the best opportunity to get a photo with them.

The well known characters from television programs are most appealing to kids. I, Krystal, have even auditioned for this position. The people in these costumes have a lot of training. Most of the time they will not talk. They will normally have a uniformed employee escorting them for crowd control and their protection.

It gets hot in the costume. If it is uncomfortably hot and humid, it is worse inside the costume. The character will signal to their helper when they need to cool off. The performers love photo-ops. If you think your child will enjoy it, take this moment to get a photos or to let your child share a hug with a favorite character.

Parades

Not every park has a parade. As a Park Hacker, I (Mike) always saw a parade as an opportunity to NOT watch the parade, but to hit certain rides while the crowd was distracted.

They are neat and I appreciate the contributions of all the performers and musicians who are in the parade. I had the opportunity to be in a marching band performing in the Magic Kingdom at Walt Disney World. I'd venture to state that I believe there is just as much, if not more, of a thrill being in the parade as there is watching one. Going from an off-stage setup area and marching into the park is a really special moment.

Fireworks

The fireworks display is one of my, Krystal's, personal favorite times of the night. At our home park, when the park closes at 10pm, and if the weather is favorable, they set off a nice display that lasts for about 5-minutes.

This is a special moment for you to pause and enjoy the park at night. It is also an inspiring moment to reflect on the fun of your whole day at the park.

Some parks offer special seating for fireworks. Ask some park employees if they have recommendations on the best areas for viewing the fireworks. Personally, I (Krystal) like watching them from the back of the park. The longer walk out is nice, because the park is quiet and I get to walk past all the rides that I enjoyed earlier.

Concerts

If you like concerts, watch the special event calendar. You will likely have several opportunities during the season to see some bands. You might get to see real bands that you actually follow. A performance at an amusement park may be a less publicized venue compared to a major headline concert. If you are into the theme of the event, take advantage of the opportunity. Because these are usually all-day special music events, you may also discover other great bands who play during the other times.

Ride Enthusiast Groups

I, Krystal, follow many of these groups on Facebook and YouTube. These groups can be local or really big national groups that span multiple home parks. You can share fan dialogue and participate in their special events.

These groups often travel to parks around the country, and around the globe. These are usually the most serious fans of roller coasters and are happy to let you pick their brain about favorite rides far away, or traits of the different manufacturers. Here is a list of a few that I follow:

- **FYE Coasters**
- **Ohio Valley Coaster**
- **Coaster Guy 101**
- **Koaster Kids**
- **American Coaster Enthusiasts** - Southern Ohio region

These are just a portion of the enthusiast groups out there. There is a good chance you may see them in your park, sporting t-shirts with their group logo. Don't forget to say hello and tell them you're a Park Hacker!

Fundraiser Events

Every park has their own charities they support. Where you have crowds and interesting events and locations available, there is no doubt you'll see events and opportunities for special fun promoted to you when you're visiting, or if you're on the park's mailing list.

Running Events - If you enjoy running an occasional 5k, 10k or half-marathon, joining an event at an amusement park might be one of your favorite races. The event usually gets you special behind-the-scenes access as the running path weaves in and out of the park.

Sometimes you get to go under and through roller coasters where guests are not normally permitted. I also saw a park's boneyard a few years ago with large scaled props from old attractions piled up. As I ran past, I could make out large fiberglass or foam characters and signage components. They were faded, but still identifiable. It was a rare treat.

You often get a special event t-shirt and a finisher's medal. These are fun events and there usually is no pressure to run competitively. I even stopped to take pictures of the backside of one of my favorite roller coasters.

Auctions - Keep an eye on your park's blog or Twitter feed. There could be auctions for all manner of things. I've seen retired props and ride seats offered for sale. I've also heard of special access events. The parks are filled with backstage secrets and interesting tour potential. If they want to dangle access to a special opportunity, like being among the first to ride a new ride, it will be sure to draw a crowd.

Special Tours - Related to the previous Auction topic, any park may decide to sell access to special tours. Indoor attraction walk-throughs, tours of maintenance areas, off-season visits and also construction tours for upcoming rides are just a few of the ways the parks can offer you a special way to see the park.

Overnights - School groups, church groups, special scout nights and even family campouts are often offered in parks around the country. If you follow their Twitter, Facebook feeds or read their blog, you'll be sure to see them coming up.

Sometimes these can get expensive. If they offer a certain amount of space and set a limit of people within that space, rather than a price per person, it might be a nice opportunity to join up with another family or bring some extra relatives to max out your space. Every event like this is different. Make sure you get a nap before you go, no sense feeling bad during the fun!

CHAPTER 7
SEASONAL EVENTS

Special Events

Every park has special events spread throughout their calendar. I like to use Holiday World as an example. They have HoliWood Nights in June. Other parks offer similar night-long events where roller coaster enthusiast groups can stay late, often riding all night.

Halloween

Halloween or Fall in general is one of my (Krystal's) favorite times of the year. This is a very exciting time in the park with the change of the atmosphere as they retheme it to be spooky. It is bittersweet, because at my home park this it the sign that the season was coming to an end.

During Halloween many parks add haunted house-style mazes and related twists to their live entertainment. Many parks split their hours to offer times for kids and times for the scary stuff.

Some rides may be closed, but most of the rides and attractions open.

Check the park website or call guest services to ask about what rides will be closed during the event.

If you're considering taking small children to these haunted events, most parks offer different options. Our home park has daytime activities which are more like costume contests, pumpkin decorating, trick-or-treat and corn maze activities. Then after dark, the tone is geared more to adults and older teens. Many parks suggest that children should be over 13 for those darker attractions, because they can be quite intense. Stage shows can also be very dark, or even overtly sexual in tone. Small children still come to these events. Even though there are many cautions posted and shared through forums, parents still choose to bring them. You should make sure to find out what is involved, so that you're prepared.

People with health conditions should use caution when going to the park during the haunt. Strobe lights, thick fog, revolving tunnel effects and other surprises can aggravate certain conditions. I, Krystal, experienced one of these. I am claustrophobic and there is one maze that is completely dark. I didn't realize exactly how pitch black it was going to be. I started to have a panic attack only five seconds in. I practically dragged my husband through one the walls to get back outside. The attendants understood what was going on and did their best to get me to calm down.

The point of this story is to share that, you may walk into something unexpected. The workers are there to help, especially if you have a medical condition. The actors will help you as well if they see something is not right.

Christmas

Several Cedar Fair parks this year are getting a special bonus to the season. It is called WinterFest. Many parks around the country also have special Christmas events. There are usually special lighting displays, seasonal food options and live shows. Our home park will be adding ice skating. Not all, but some of the park's rides may be operating.

These can be very special events, heavy in the holiday atmosphere and ambiance. Check the list of attractions and options to make sure you have the right idea of what areas of the park are open.

Special Theme Weeks

This is a small tip, because it generally won't affect the main aspects of the park. If you watch the social media and the blogs, you may spot a fun themed week. A couple years ago we had a Christmas in July week. It was a fun departure from normal, with Christmas music playing inside the main entrance.

Parks create and add surprising special events all season long. Some might be light and others might be among the best moments you spend in the park all season!

CHAPTER 8
ADD YOUR OWN FUN

It is human nature to get bored. It is hard to imagine when you first visit a park, that if you were to visit it twenty or thirty times in a season, that the excitement would diminish. It isn't the park's fault, you've just saturated yourself to the point where it feels like ride - ride - ride, etc.

Starting with a quick reminder to keep your play within the rules of the park, followed by encouragement to always be courteous to employees and other park visitors, it is now time to get creative!

Gamification

Bucket List

At the start of the season, or on a one-day visit to a park that is new to you, you want to decide what you want to ride. Creating a bucket list will help keep your goal in front of you. It also helps ensure you don't realize on your way home, or at the end of the season, that you overlooked a ride.

You have the freedom to create your own bucket list. It is the list of attractions that you intend to complete. If you visit multiple parks, you might be working to ride all of a certain kind of ride, perhaps all the rides from one of those manufacturers. You may also want to ride every coaster that does inversions, an upside-down bucket list, if you will.

Autographs

We've talked about helping your kids through the adventure of meeting the costumed characters and the live performers. This can also become a game as you work to help them collect autographs from all the cast of a show, or to meet every character.

If you're a fan of a particular amusement park, you can also collect moments meeting with some of their senior leaders as they walk the park. You can often spot someone who is in a management role at a park, their uniforms are a little different. They are usually friendly and courteous. If you spot someone who looks important, it might be educational, if they don't look extremely busy, to say hello and ask them what they do at the park.

Top Rides

If a person is an amusement park or roller coaster enthusiast, it stands to reason that they are wanting to ride on all the high profile rides. Some count the number of times they've ridden roller coasters in their life. Others collect the experience of riding different roller coasters.

It is a little like the bucket list, but your list keeps growing more like you are collecting the experiences of each ride.

Personal Challenge and Growth

If you have a phobia or are hesitant about riding a certain kind of ride, you may decide to take conquering that obstacle as a personal challenge or an opportunity for growth.

Loops/Inversions - Once you get locked into the ride, you've made a big step. You can work your way up by riding through those sections with your eyes closed, then looking straight forward, and finally looking around during the loop.

Heights - I addressed dealing with a fear of heights at the end of chapter 5. If you have a serious, debilitating phobia, I (Mike) don't intend to make you uncomfortable or cause you personal harm. If it is a desire of yours to ride the tall rides, I want to help you reach those goals. From the ground, the rides are clearly strong, like a tall building. The views of the park from those heights are fantastic!

Maybe it will be easier to venture up there on a space needle or tower attraction with an observation deck. It might also be possible that doing it as a ride, would offer some distraction from the height. Think about what aspect it is that you fear and explore ways of working around that issue.

Parkaeology

… or would it be Parchaeology? Park + archaeology, whatever! Discovering clues and evidence of attractions from the past.

If you consider yourself an amateur sleuth, or fancy a geocaching expedition, then this "game" may be right up your alley. Discovering elements of extinct attractions, is an exciting thing to do at any amusement park. There are subtle clues to find an old ride location.

The first step is to print an old map of the park. You can find these using Google and by exploring the park enthusiast forums. These maps can show how the park used to be laid out. Sometimes rides are completely erased, with new rides completely covering the old evidence. Other times, there is evidence left behind.

Look for walking paths that lead to nowhere. This could be an entrance to the queue or even an actual track for an old ride. By looking at the ground, you may even spot old queue post holes that have been filled-in.

One of my favorite things to spot, are old, unused concrete footers. These large concrete blocks are harder to move and are often worked around. Some parks won't take them out which gives you solid evidence of the location for parts of a ride's structure.

The last way, which is easy and also very fun, is when the park management pull old cars out to make a special appearance during an event like a Halloween decoration.

Some trains can also be spotted during backstage VIP tours. Sometime the haunted mazes use old ride buildings. If you look around, you can see elements and decorations that were part of the ride.

Recreate a Photo

If you have visited a certain park during your childhood, you can build a fun tradition of posing in the same location every year and repeating the photo. Beside the fact that everyone is older than in the previous photo, rides and scenery also change, so that may offer some additional challenges.

You can also mimic a photo of your family's previous generation. If you were the child in the photo before, you can retake the same image with you as the parent and your kids can pose where you were in the past.

Television Program or Movie Locations

With our home park being Kings Island, we have special historical reference of the park in the form of episodes of Brady Bunch and The Partridge Family both being filmed there. These special episodes were both during the early years of the park to help promote the new amusement park.

Today, a great deal of the park is different, but that creates the fun challenge. Watch the episodes and identify what is in certain locations now, if they are different. You can reenact scenes and shoot a photo as an homage to the episode.

Here are some other famous movies filmed in parks you can visit today:

> **National Lampoon's Vacation** – Six Flags Magic Mountain (as Walley World)
> **Big, The Muppets Take Manhattan, Fatal Attraction, Final Destination 3** and **Sweet and Lowdown** – Rye Playland
> **Rollercoaster** – Six Flags Magic Mountain
> **Beverly Hills Cop III** – California's Great America
> **Jaws 3-D** – SeaWorld Orlando
> **Jurassic World** – Six Flags New Orleans
> **Adventureland** – Kennywood
> **House on Haunted Hill** – Islands of Adventure
> **Zombieland** – Wild Adventures/Scream Fest Theme Park
> **The Littlest Hobo** - Canada's Wonderland

TV programs:

> **Brady Bunch** – Kings Island
> **The Partridge Family** – Kings Island
> **Are You Afraid of the Dark** – Six Flags LaRonde Canada
> **3 Ninjas: High Noon at Mega Mountain** – Elitch Gardens

If we missed any, let us know on the website by using the Share-A-Hack form. We know that nearly every sitcom, especially ABC sitcoms, have episodes that travel to Walt Disney World.

Boosting a Ride

Some of these variations have been covered in the Special Modifications section of chapter 5. There are ways to produce a variety of experiences on thrill rides. All seats usually provide a great experience with similar sensations. If you want to shake it up a little, here are some ways you can dial-up the fun!

Eyes Shut - Some riders close their eyes out of fear. If you're not one of those people, you can create a very different experience by denying yourself the visual cues of what is coming next. Even a dark ride can be made to feel very different, even scarier, by riding it with your eyes closed.

Exploit the Unexpected - If a roller coaster has a twin, where two trains race and the tracks either mirror each other or follow slightly different tracks, you can fool yourself by doing one track several times in a row and then switching to the other side. This can also be changed further by combining this Park Hack with the previous one. Your eyes are closed and your body is expecting a turn to the right, but it doesn't! It goes left instead!

You can also use this strategy by repeating a roller coaster in the front of the train for a few rides, before switching to the back, or vice versa.

As mentioned in chapter 5, you can also sit on the left of a wider roller coaster for a few times and before switching to the right side.

Feet Up - If you want to increase the wildness of a ride that already throws you around, you can pull your feet up off the floor. This works well with rougher wooden coasters and the classic Arrow rides like Vortex and Corkscrew. The track pipes aren't as perfectly shaped as today's modern roller coasters. So when it transitions into a turn, the shift can be harsh. You don't realize how much your feet help to hold you in place, until you ride with them held up. Don't worry, the shoulder restraint will keep you in.

At Night - Any outdoor roller coaster creates a very different experience when it is dark. At our home park, we have a couple special wooden coasters that travel through the woods. Add darkness and the thrill increases a great deal!

Track Your Steps

With today's technology there are many ways to track of how much you walk. I, Krystal, do most of my walking at the park. I often average 10 miles during a visit. I realize, sometimes it is a fluke because my phone may also count my movement on rides. If your smartphone has a health or fitness app, it can track your steps.

Another popular way to track steps, is by wearing an activity bracelet, like a Fitbit. When you get to the park, take note of your step total. Then compare it at the end of the park visit. You will be surprised by how much you can walk at the park.

BECOME A PARK HACKER

If you don't already follow Park Hacks, we'd like to invite you to join the conversation on **amusement.parkhacks.com**. There you will soon find FREE downloads, links to other Park Hack activities, and a form to join our email newsletter for other Park Hack tips, as shared by other Park Hackers.

You can also find us on Facebook **@amusementparkhacks** or by going to: **https://www.facebook.com/amusementparkhacks/**.

If you have a friend or family who is an amusement park or roller coaster enthusiast, please share these links with them. They may have valuable insight to add for their park.

The main purpose of this book is to help ensure that visitors to the park have a fun visit. That may mean families with small children, who may know how to manage a visit to the park with small children. There are others who may think the park is just an expensive, crowded place with noise and bad food. They may have had a bad experience and ruled out future opportunities for fun at the park for their children. We want these tips to help them give amusement parks another try. There are beautiful, quiet evenings when the sun is setting and the park takes on a magical appearance. Encourage these people to check out our Park Hacks, so they too can discover what we love about these parks.

INDEX OF AMUSEMENT PARKS

When I decided to expand the Park Hacks brand from my home park of Kings Island to the many other parks around North America, I was stunned how many parks there were! Of course there are also nice parks all around the globe, but for this version of the book, and expansion to the parks of America or North America, which can include Canada and Mexico, as well as the US, is already a pretty formidable list to make.

If your park is not listed here, send us a note. You can use the Share-A-Hack form, or write me directly at mike@parkhacks.com.

Cedar Fair

Cedar Fair Main Site - https://www.cedarfair.com/

California Great America - Santa Clara, CA
www.cagreatamerica.com

Canada's Wonderland - Vaughan, Ontario
www.canadaswonderland.com

Carowinds - Charlotte, NC
www.carowinds.com

Cedar Point - Sandusky, OH
www.cedarpoint.com

Cedar Point Shores - Sandusky, OH
www.cedarpoint.com/play/cedar-point-shores

Dorney Park & Wildwater Kingdom - Allentown, PA
www.dorneypark.com

Kings Dominion - Doswell, VA
www.kingsdominion.com

Kings Island - Kings Mills, OH
www.visitkingsisland.com

Knott's Berry Farm - Buena Park, CA
www.knotts.com

Knott's Soak City Waterpark - Buena Park, CA
www.knotts.com/play/soak-city

Michigan's Adventure - Muskegon, MI
www.miadventure.com

Valley Fair - Shakopee, MN
www.valleyfair.com

Worlds of Fun / Oceans of Fun - Kansas City, MO
www.worldsoffun.com

Six Flags

Six Flags Main Site - www.sixflags.com

California

Six Flags Discovery Kingdom - Vallejo, CA (near San Francisco)
www.sixflags.com/discoverykingdom

Water World - Concord, CA
waterworldcalifornia.com

Six Flags Magic Mountain - Los Angeles, CA
www.sixflags.com/magicmountain

Six Flags Hurricane Harbor - Los Angeles, CA
www.sixflags.com/hurricaneharborla

Georgia

Six Flags Over Georgia - Atlanta, GA
www.sixflags.com/overGeorgia

Six Flags White Water - Atlanta, GA
www.sixflags.com/whiteWater

Illinois

Six Flags Great America - Chicago, IL
www.sixflags.com/greatAmerica

Maryland

Six Flags America - Baltimore/Washington, DC
www.sixflags.com/america

Massachusetts

Six Flags New England - Agawam, MA
www.sixflags.com/newEngland

Missouri

Six Flags St. Louis - St. Louis, MO
www.sixflags.com/stLouis

New Jersey

Six Flags Great Adventure - Jackson, NJ
www.sixflags.com/greatAdventure

Six Flags Hurricane Harbor - Jackson, NJ
www.sixflags.com/hurricaneHarborNJ

New York

Great Escape - Lake George, NY
www.sixflags.com/greatEscape

Six Flags Great Escape Lodge & Indoor Waterpark - Lake George, NY
www.sixflagsgreatescapelodge.com

Texas

Six Flags Fiesta Texas - San Antonio, TX
www.sixflags.com/fiestaTexas

Six Flags Over Texas - Arlington, TX
www.sixflags.com/overTexas

Six Flags Hurricane Harbor - Arlington, TX
www.sixflags.com/hurricaneHarborTexas

Canada

Six Flags - La Ronde - Montreal, Quebec
www.laronde.com/larondeen

Mexico

Six Flags Mexico - Mexico City, Mexico
www.sixflags.com/mexico

Hurricane Harbor Oaxtepec - Oaxtepec, Mexico
www.sixflags.com/hurricaneharbormx

(Although this book concentrates on North America, Six Flags has two more parks on other continents!)

China

Six Flags Haiyan - Zhejiang, China
www.sixflags.com/haiyan

United Arab Emirates

Six Flags Dubai - Dubai, UAE
www.sixflags.com/dubai

SeaWorld

SeaWorld Parks and Entertainment Main Site
seaworldparks.com

Discovery Cove - Orlando, FL
discoverycove.com

SeaWorld Orlando - Orlando, FL
seaworld.com/orlando

SeaWorld San Diego - San Diego, CA
seaworld.com/san-diego

SeaWorld San Antonio - San Antonio, TX
seaworld.com/san-antonio

Sesame Place - Philadelphia, PA
sesameplace.com/philadelphia

Busch Gardens

Busch Gardens Tampa - Tampa, FL
buschgardens.com/tampa/

Busch Gardens Williamsburg - Williamsburg, VA
seaworldparks.com/en/buschgardens-williamsburg

Schlitterbahn Waterparks

Galveston, TX
www.schlitterbahn.com/galveston

New Braunfels, TX
www.schlitterbahn.com/new-braunfels

South Padre Island, TX
www.schlitterbahn.com/south-padre-island

Corpus Christi, TX
www.schlitterbahn.com/corpus-christi

Kansas City, Kansas
www.schlitterbahn.com/kansas-city

Independent Parks

Colorado

Elitch Gardens - Denver, CO
elitchgardens.com

Santa's Workshop - Cascade, Colorado
northpolecolorado.com

Idaho

Silverwood & Boulder Beach - Athol, ID
www.silverwoodthemepark.com

Indiana

Holiday World & Splashin' Safari - Santa Claus, Indiana
www.holidayworld.com

Iowa

Adventureland - Altoona, IA
www.adventurelandresort.com

Kentucky

Kentucky Kingdom - Louisville, KY
www.kentuckykingdom.com

Massachusetts

Edaville Family Theme Park - South Carver, MA
www.edaville.com

Minnesota

Nickelodeon Universe at the Mall of America
- Bloomington, MN - nickelodeonuniverse.com

Missouri

Silver Dollar City - Branson, MO
www.silverdollarcity.com/theme-park

Nevada

Circus Circus Adventuredome - Las Vegas, NV
www.circuscircus.com/en/adventuredome.html

New Hampshire

Canobie Lake Park - Salem, NH
www.canobie.com

New York

NY Coney Island - Brooklyn, NY
lunaparknyc.com/attractions/cyclone

Rye Playland - Rye, NY
playlandpark.org

Darien Lake - Darien Center, NY
www.darienlake.com

Pennsylvania

Dutch Wonderland - Lancaster, PA
www.dutchwonderland.com

Hershey Park - Hershey, PA
www.hersheypark.com

Kennywood - West Mifflin, PA
www.kennywood.com

Idlewild & SoakZone - Ligonier, PA
www.idlewild.com

Knoebels - Elysburg, PA
www.knoebels.com

Tennessee

Lake Winnie - Chattanooga, TN
www.lakewinnie.com

Dollywood - Pigeon Forge, TN
www.dollywood.com

West Virginia

Camden Park - Huntington, WV
www.camdenpark.com

Other Amusement Attractions

The above is not exhaustive, but a good attempt at listing the major, and even a few smaller amusement parks. One of our focus group Park Hackers reviewing the material for this book, Jean Lines from Columbus, Ohio, reminded me that there are many tourist areas that may not immediately be considered an amusement park, but there are many attractions in a collected tourist area that share many traits of amusement parks. These may be great places to build a lot of similar memories for your family.

Coastal towns on both Atlantic and Pacific coasts often have boardwalk areas with many amusement park attractions:

Myrtle Beach, SC
www.familykingdomfun.com

Wildwood, NJ
www.moreyspiers.com
and www.wildwoodsnj.com/wildwood-attractions.cfm

Rye, NY (See Rye Playland mentioned above)

Santa Cruz, CA
beachboardwalk.com

Vallejo, CA (See Six Flags Discovery Kingdom mentioned above)

Santa Monica Pier, CA
www.pacpark.com

Sandusky, OH (See Cedar Point mentioned above)

Hampton Beach, NH
www.hamptonbeachcasinonh.com

Rehoboth Beach, DE
www.funlandrehoboth.com

New York, NY
lunaparknyc.com
and www.wonderwheel.com (New York's Coney Island)

Cincinnati, OH (On the Ohio River)
coneyislandpark.com

San Diego, CA
www.belmontpark.com
and www.legoland.com/california

Newport Beach, CA
www.balboaferriswheel.com

Atlantic City, NJ
www.steelpier.com

Ocean City, MD
www.trimpersrides.com
and www.ocbound.com/ocean-city-md/things-to-do/

Rehoboth Beach, DE
www.funlandrehoboth.com

Virginia Beach, VA
www.atlanticfunpark.com

Other inland tourist areas

There are also areas like these boardwalks where many attractions develop. Places like Gatlinburg and Pigeon Forge, TN and Branson, MO have large amusement parks nearby. These are also similar to the boardwalks above where independent rides and attractions can be visited, that aren't contained within the bounds of one park management company.

THANK YOU

On behalf of my co-author Krystal, all of the focus group, the other active Park Hackers and myself, I'd like to thank you for reading this 2018 edition of Amusement Park Hacks. The Park Hacks series is intended to be updated annually. If you see anything you disagree with, or doesn't reflect a park that you visit, please let us know.

Also, if you found these tips to be helpful, especially for new amusement park enthusiasts and parents figuring out how to make sure a trip to the park is a blast, please take a moment and give it a review and a five-star rating on Amazon or whatever fine bookstore you found it.

Anyone can be a Park Hacker. If you want to join the ongoing community, check out the blog: **http://amusement.parkhacks.com** and sign-up for the email list.

I hope to see you at the park! If you spot me, please say "hello!"
—Mike Kunze